American College of Cardiology

A Visual History

1949 – 1999

Library of Congress
Catalog Card Number: 98-74461

American College of Cardiology
A Visual History 1949 – 1999
Copyright © 1998
American College of Cardiology
ISBN 1-892895-74-9

American College of Cardiology
9111 Old Georgetown Road
Bethesda, Maryland 20814-1699

Designed by CONTEXT, Inc.
South Norwalk, CT

Printed in Italy by Amilcare Pizzi S.p.A.

Contents

Foreword 4

Introduction 5

The Legacy 7

Formation of the ACC 17

Vision to Reality 29

The Turning Point 41

Prosperity 51

New Issues, New Ways 63

ACC: A Portrait 75

Afterword 86

Acknowledgments 88

Foreword

The last 50 years have seen the world of cardiology develop with a definite American accent. The acceptance of new ideas and the rejection of ineffective methods have characterized the explosive growth of our profession for the benefit of our patients. What we see today is highly sophisticated technology, but what underlies that technology is a free flow of ideas exchanged openly.

The American College of Cardiology, the world's leading cardiology educational institution, was founded by immigrants emerging from a very different European system. Created in controversy, the ACC has emerged as a true partner with the American Heart Association to facilitate the emergence of cardiology as a preeminent discipline in modern medicine.

The exponential growth of knowledge in our discipline is not unlike the opening of the American West or space exploration. The ACC has been at the forefront of disseminating this knowledge. Through practice guidelines and consensus statements, effective therapies have been applied more consistently. Impediments to implementing high-quality care are constantly monitored by the ACC's advocacy mission. Efforts to bring governments and the private sector payers to the common goal of quality care and prevention for our patients is an ongoing commitment of the ACC. Most important, the College provides the forum for educational excellence. Who will educate us, the practitioners, about the opportunities for disease control arising from the Human Genome Project unless it is the ACC? Now, as we celebrate 50 years of accomplishments in the battle against cardiovascular disease, we must look forward to the even greater opportunities of the next 50 years. In doing so, we must not forget the lessons of the past. America, the melting pot of races, creeds, and religions, has also become the melting pot of ideas. If cardiology and the American College of Cardiology are to flourish and achieve our stated goals, the spirit of adventure that launched the College must be instilled in the next generation of explorers who, I am confident, will surpass even the accomplishments that amaze us today.

Spencer B. King III

Spencer B. King III, MD, FACC
President, American College of Cardiology

Introduction

Two generations of cardiologists – from North America and around the world – have looked to the American College of Cardiology for timely and accurate information about advances in the diagnosis and treatment of patients with cardiovascular disease. For half a century, the College has facilitated meaningful interaction among practitioners, researchers, educators, and representatives of industry and the federal government. Their complementary roles in creating, disseminating, and using new knowledge as well as pharmaceutical and technological innovations resulted in many dramatic advances in patient care. This volume celebrates the past, present, and future of the American College of Cardiology in pictures and words. It closes with a photo essay that depicts some of our stakeholders, images meant to convey the rich intellectual and professional diversity of contemporary cardiovascular medicine and surgery. May Roustom and many other ACC staff members assisted Context and writer, Charles Rhudy, to create this historical record. I had the privilege of serving with former College presidents H. Jeremy C. Swan, John F. Williams, Jr., and William L. Winters, Jr., on a working group that helped bring the project to fruition.

Bruce Fye

W. Bruce Fye, MD, MA, FACC
Historian, American College of Cardiology

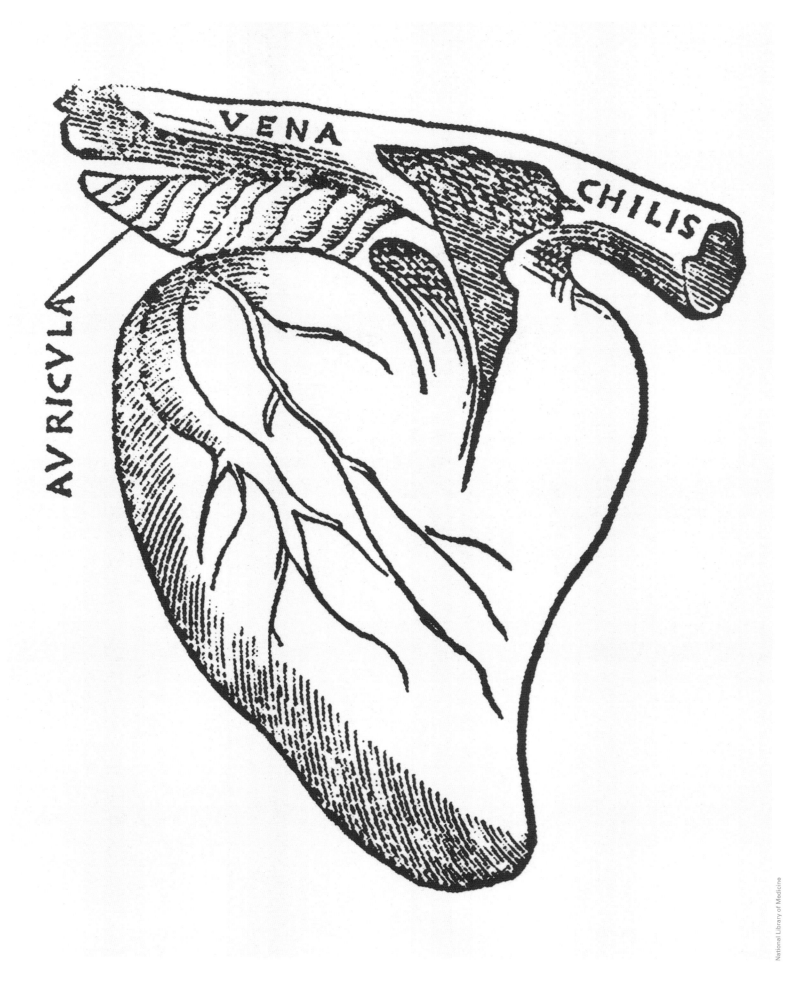

VENA

CHILIS

AVRICVLA

Jacopo Berengario de Carpi
(ca. 1460 – 1530) was the first
anatomist to publish illustrations
of a dissected heart.

The Legacy

Throughout history, all societies have possessed medical beliefs. Early civilizations believed that life could be explained by the natural world of celestial bodies, mountains and forests, rivers and seas, as well as by the favor or displeasure of the gods. In time, humans came to understand that natural laws ruled the world. Renaissance medicine focused on the body, and anatomical and physiological inquiries led investigators to deeper levels of understanding. In 1315, Mondino de Luzzi, who held the chair of medicine at the University of Padua, authored the first comprehensive anatomy text. More than two centuries later, in 1543, a Paduan professor, Andreas Vesalius, published a landmark anatomical work, *De Humani Corporis Fabrica*. Coming at the high tide of the Renaissance, this work galvanized the intellectual community, and Vesalius inspired scientific zeal in students for years to come. In 1628, William Harvey published *De Motu Cordis* demonstrating the circulation of blood and the heart's role as a pump. Perhaps the most enduring contribution of Harvey's book, however, was that it was based on visible, practical experiments. Over the centuries, progress came on many fronts – albeit with painful slowness. The microscope was developed, and the laboratory emerged. In the late 18th century, digitalis was discovered. In the 19th century, the stethoscope was developed, and X-rays were discovered. In the latter part of the century, there arose a group of physicians who focused on the heart. They joined the ranks of other emerging specialties, such as ophthalmology, gynecology, and radiology. In 1902, a new medical tool appeared – Einthoven's electrocardiograph, the first practical, direct method of tracing the heart's electrical activity. Suddenly, the practitioners of a new discipline had a unique tool to differentiate themselves. The stage was set. The first century of cardiology lay ahead.

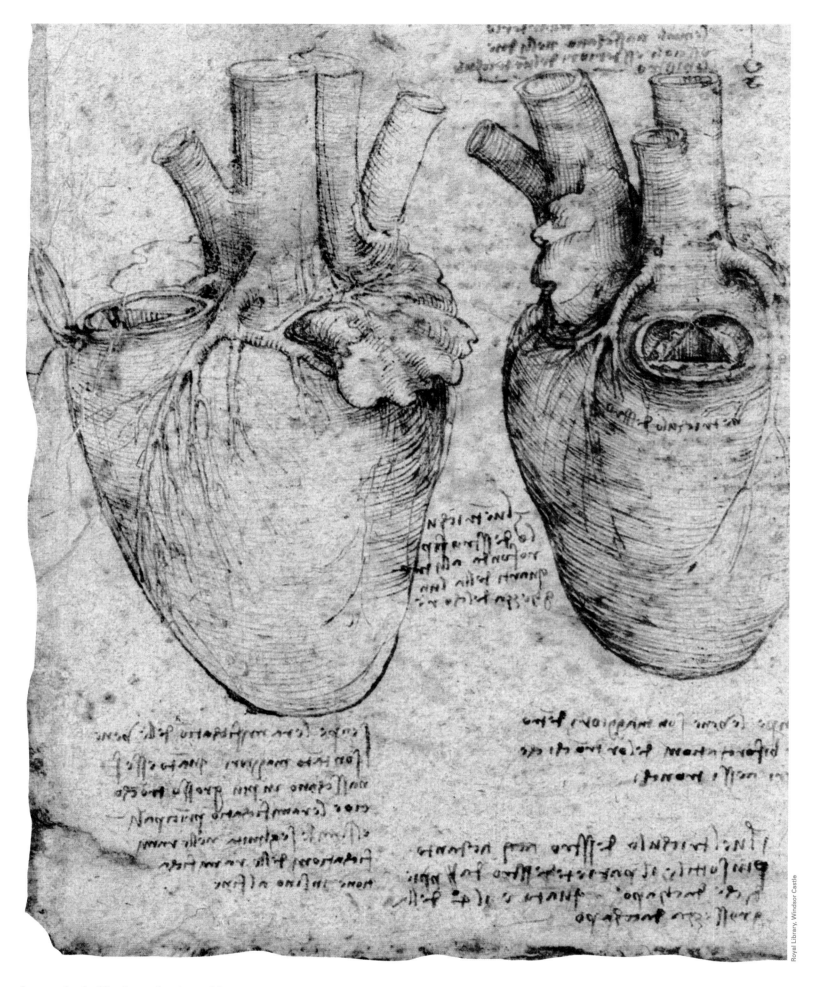

Leonardo da Vinci was fascinated by
the workings of the heart, and his
drawings of the coronary arteries were
remarkable for their accuracy.

1772

William Heberden publishes his classic description

of angina pectoris

1785

William Withering publishes his monograph on foxglove

(digitalis) as a remedy for dropsy

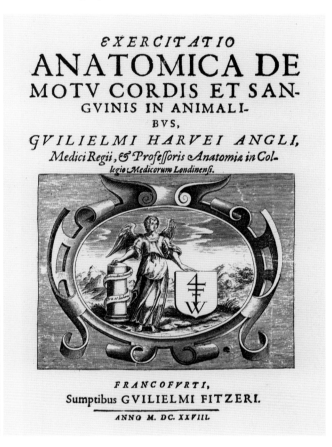

1819

René Läennec publishes his book on auscultation that includes his

invention of the stethoscope

1895

Wilhelm Röentgen discovers X-rays

1912

James Herrick publishes his classic description of acute

myocardial infarction

The ACC's logo is derived from a landmark
anatomical work, *De Humani Corporis Fabrica*, by
Andreas Vesalius, which was published in 1543.

In 1628, William Harvey's *De Motu Cordis* first
demonstrated the circulation of blood and the
heart's role as a pump.

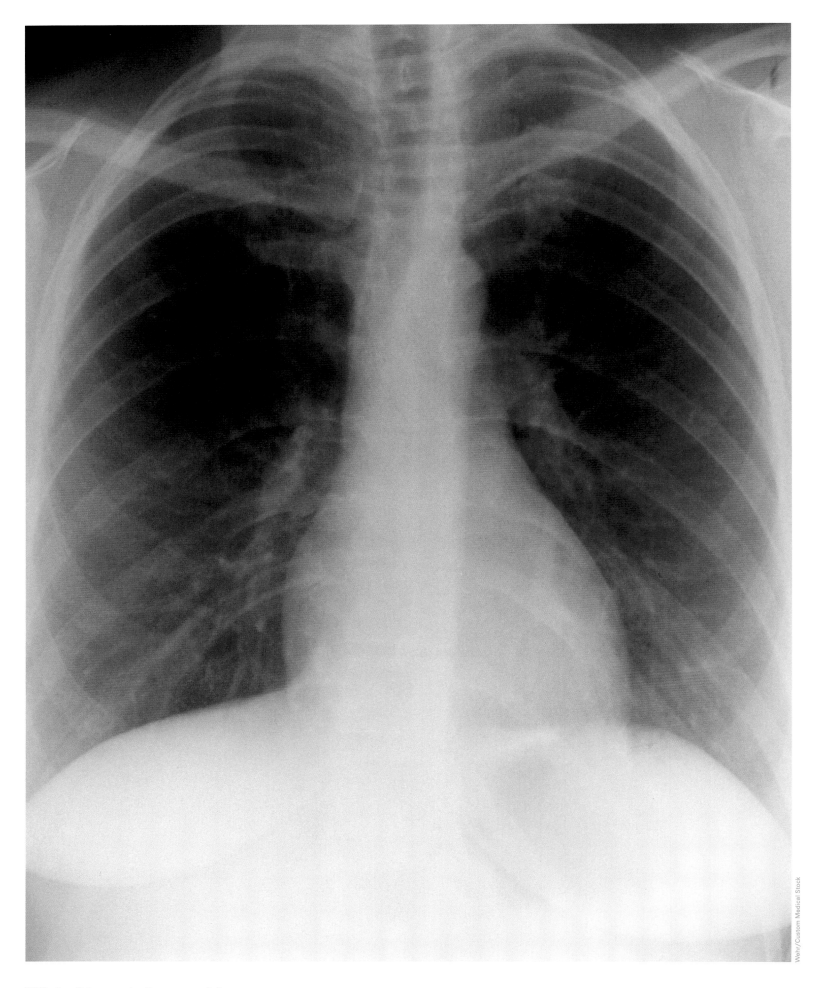

Wilhelm Röentgen's discovery of the
X-ray in 1895 made it possible to
take pictures of internal body structures
on film.

1929

Werner Forssmann performs the first documented human
cardiac catheterization, on himself

1948

Dwight Harken and Charles Bailey report surgical procedures
to relieve mitral stenosis

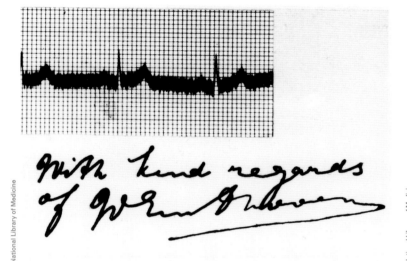

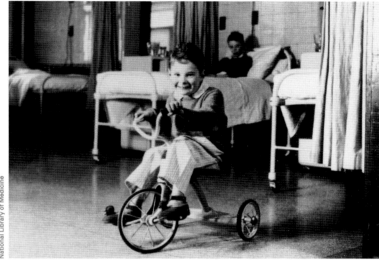

National Library of Medicine

1948

The Framingham Heart Study, the first major effort to study the
epidemiology of chronic disease, is launched

1954

Inge Edler and Carl Helmuth Hertz report using ultrasound to
image the beating heart in humans (echocardiography)

1958

Mason Sones performs the first selective coronary arteriogram

1960

Richard Lower and Norman Shumway report the first
successful orthotopic homotransplantation of a canine heart

In 1902, William Einthoven's electrocardiograph
emerged as the first practical, direct method of
tracing the heart's electrical activity.

The success of Alfred Blalock's "blue-baby operation" in 1944 opened a new era in the treatment of
cardiovascular disease.

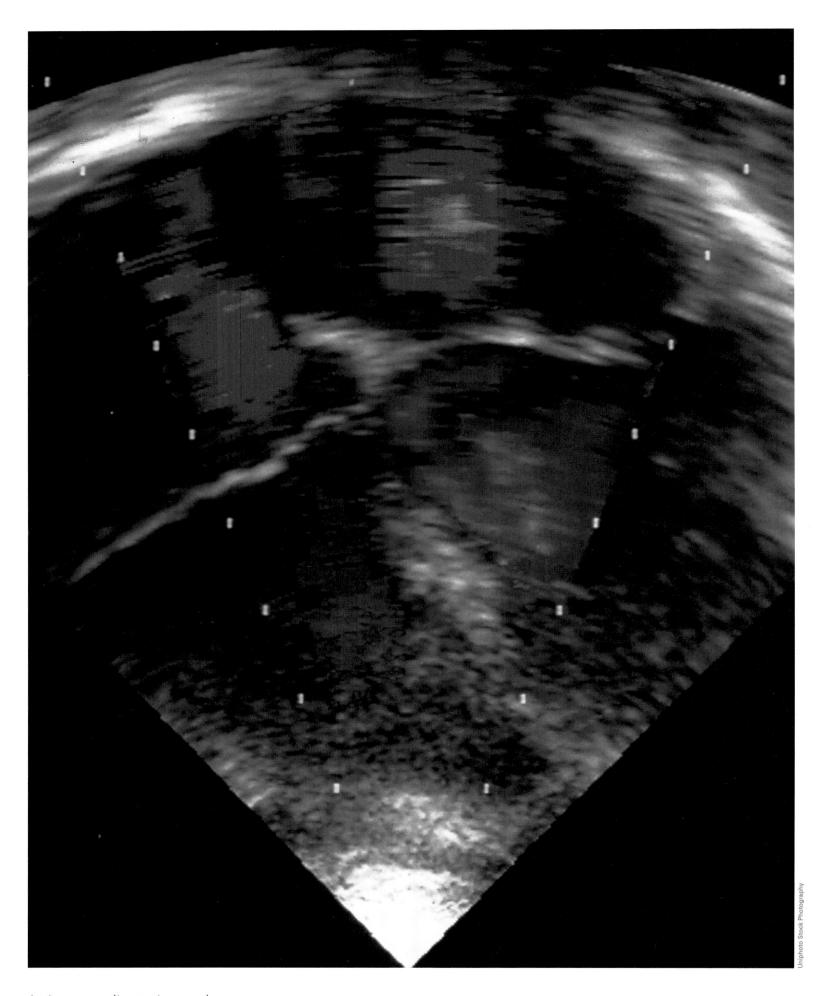

An important diagnostic procedure.
echocardiography. uses high frequency
sound waves – similar to radar or
sonar – to record moving pictures of
the heart.

1961

The Framingham Heart Study finds that cholesterol level, blood pressure,
and electrocardiogram abnormalities increase the risk of heart disease

1968

René Favaloro reports saphenous vein coronary artery bypass
graft surgery (CABG) for angina pectoris

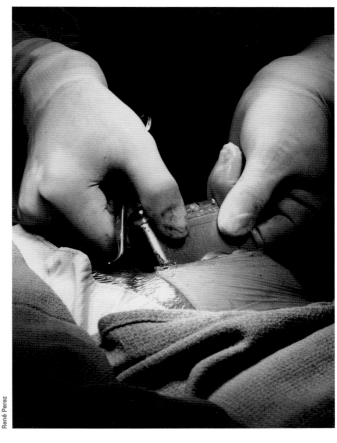

1976

E.I. Cházov et al. report the successful reperfusion
of an infarct-related artery with intracoronary streptokinase
in a patient with an acute myocardial infarction

1977

Andreas Grüntzig reports percutaneous transluminal coronary
angioplasty (PTCA)

Philadelphia surgeon John Gibbon, Jr., developed
the heart-lung machine to oxygenate the blood
during intracardiac surgery.

Implantation of electronic cardiac pacemakers, first
achieved in 1960, was a breakthrough in the
treatment of patients with symptomatic heart block.

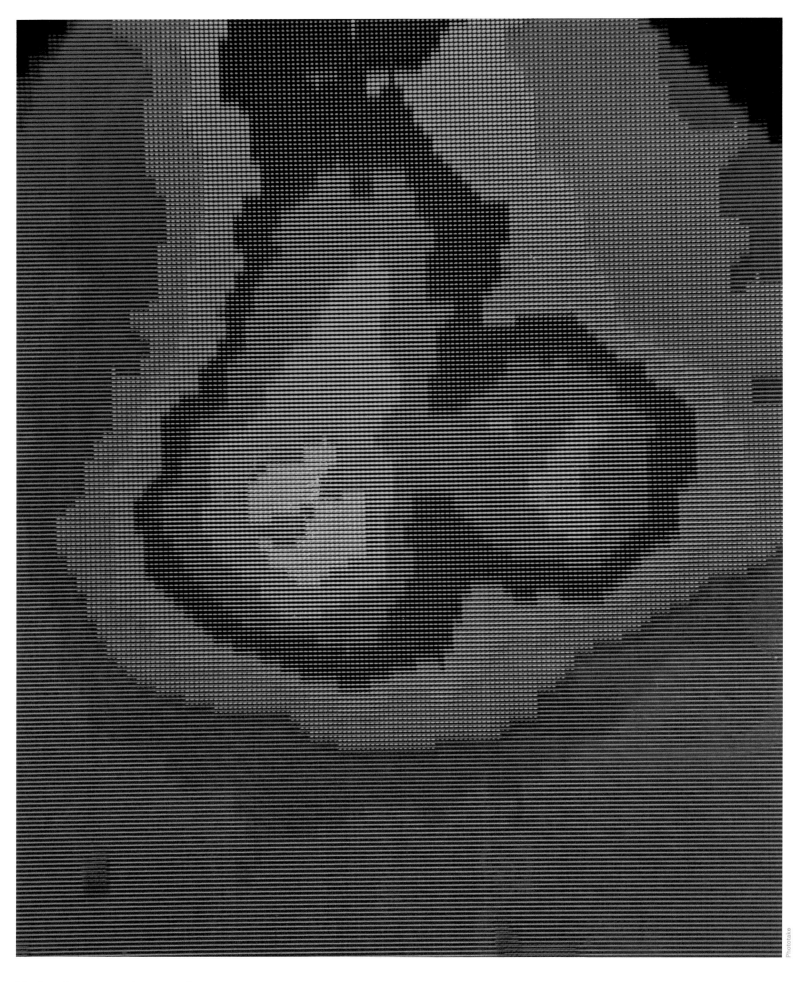

Nuclear heart scanning – involving
injection of radioactive "tracers" into
the bloodstream – is used to show
features of the heart and blood flow.

1980

Michael Mirowski reports treating malignant ventricular arrhyth-
mias in humans with an implanted automatic defibrillator

1982

William DeVries performs the first artificial
heart surgery

Genentech, Inc.

1986

Jacques Puel and Ulrich Sigwart insert the first stent in a human
coronary artery

1991

Warren M. Jackman publishes his article showing that radio-
frequency current is highly effective in ablating atrioventricular
pathways in Wolff-Parkinson-White syndrome

Timothy D. Henry presents his finding that the
protein vascular endothelial growth factor
(VEGF) could prompt new blood vessel growth
on the heart at the ACC's March 1998 Annual
Scientific Session in Atlanta.

Einthoven's string galvanometer.
known as the electrocardiograph. gave
practitioners of cardiology a
device that set their discipline apart.

Formation of the ACC

On the Sunday after Thanksgiving 1949, the New York City area tasted the season's first snow – a few inches that added an unwelcome dimension to the rigors of driving home after a long holiday weekend.

In the storm's wake, the following day, November 28, was cloudy and cold. *The New York Times* quoted Allied spokesmen as saying they had no intention of rearming Germany. Chinese Communist troops were closing in on Chungking. The weekend editorials had spoken of a nation thankful for peace and prosperity.

On that Monday, an organizational meeting of the "American College of Cardiologists" was held in the Park Avenue office of Franz Groedel. Groedel chaired the meeting, during which a draft constitution was presented, revised, and signed by 14 physicians. One of the founders' first acts was to hire a lawyer to "secure the name American College of Cardiologists in the District of Columbia."

A few days later, on December 2, the "American College of Cardiology" was granted a corporate charter in Washington, D.C. On December 6, the "American College of Cardiologists, Inc." was chartered in Delaware.

Although now a mere footnote to history, the ACC began life with two names as a legal precaution to prevent a group with a similar name from securing a charter of its own. This dual identity lasted precisely one year, until December 2, 1950, when the Board of Trustees of the American College of Cardiology met in New York and a single organization emerged.

Like most newly founded organizations, the ACC faced an uncertain future. Perhaps because it was and is an organization of, by, and for cardiovascular specialists – no strangers to challenge – the organization not only survived, it flourished.

Franz M. Groedel, MD
ACC President, 1949 – 1951

In addition to Groedel, who was president of the new society, the signatories to the draft constitution were Philip Reichert, secretary-treasurer; Max Miller, assistant secretary; and 11 members of the New York Cardiological Society (NYCS). The NYCS had been founded more than two decades earlier, in 1928. Reichert described the NYCS as "a small group, but…earnest to learn what there was to know about their special subject." Even then, there were visions of a national organization of cardiovascular specialists, but the tight-knit group confined itself geographically and, according to Reichert, its members were "satisfied with what they had." Nevertheless, in the NYCS were the seeds of something far larger. What that something would become began to emerge as the NYCS matured during the 1930s and 1940s and sharpened its focus on service to practicing cardiologists and on continuing, postgraduate education – needs that were not being addressed adequately by other organizations of the era.

Groedel had been among the first in the wave of physicians to emigrate to America after Hitler's rise to power, arriving in New York in 1934. Fluent in English and widely known in medical circles after earlier professional visits to the United States, Groedel established a practice and was appointed head of cardiology at Beth David Hospital in New York City. In Europe, Groedel had been held in high esteem, but – no longer an ocean removed – he was also

ACC Founders Plaque, 1949. Founders featured in four columns are (left to right), first column: Samuel Korry, Hannibal De Bellis, Epaminonda Secondari, Attilio Robertiello; second column: Gabriel F. Greco, Samuel Blinder; third column: Bruno Kisch, Philip Reichert; fourth column: Joseph B. Wolfe, Seymour Fiske, Max Miller, Albert S. Hyman. The medal (center) carries the image of Franz Groedel.

perceived as a competitor. Reichert, already a practicing cardiologist in New York when Groedel arrived, knew of Groedel by reputation. Groedel had written extensively on cardiology, and Reichert was friendly with a leading New York cardiologist, Louis Bishop, and his son, both of whom had visited Groedel in Germany.

In 1945, the two physicians were admitted to the NYCS and in short order Groedel became its president and Reichert its secretary and treasurer. Dissatisfied with the perceived shortcomings of other organizations and holding fast to the earlier vision of a national organization of cardiologists, the two were ideally positioned to form a new society and recruit their colleagues for membership – which they did by inviting the trustees of the NYCS to become part of the founding group. Eleven responded. So it was on that wintry Monday in November 1949 that Groedel, Reichert, Miller, and 11 others met to form the American College of Cardiology.

Bruno Kisch, MD
ACC President, 1951 – 1953

At the time of the ACC's founding, the American Heart Association (AHA), which had been in existence since 1924, was the preeminent national organization for cardiovascular specialists of all descriptions. Why was it, then, that Groedel and the others felt compelled to create a new organization? On a personal level, Groedel resented the fact that, despite his distinguished record, he was not accepted by the AHA's inner circle. He, along with many other immigrant physicians, found it difficult to establish themselves in a nation wracked by the Great Depression, and they were viewed as unneeded competition by the existing medical establishment. Groedel was not alone in his dissatisfaction with the AHA. In the early 1940s, the academic and physiological cardiologists who dominated the AHA's leadership proposed an exclusive "Scientific Council" separate and apart from the AHA's general membership. Although the proposal was not implemented until 1948, it was seen by the AHA's practicing cardiologists, including Groedel, as elitist and restrictive. Moreover, the idea and subsequent creation of the council served to exacerbate the long-held view that the AHA was not sensitive to the needs of the practitioner cardiologist. Finally,

Robert P. Glover, MD
ACC President, 1953 – 1954

Ashton Graybiel, MD
ACC President, 1954 – 1955

An ACC regional meeting in New York City in 1957
was attended by some 2,500 physicians – an
indicator of the tremendous momentum gained by
the College in the decade following its founding.

many cardiologists were disappointed when, also in 1948, the AHA was transformed into a voluntary health organization whose membership would henceforth include nurses, social workers, and others.

On the positive side, the founding of the ACC could hardly have taken place at a more fortuitous time, occurring, as it did, on the threshold of what Eugene Braunwald, writing in *An Era in Cardiovascular Medicine*, called "The Golden Age of Cardiology." On June 16, 1948, President Harry Truman signed the National Heart Act, which established the National Heart Institute (NHI, now the National Heart, Lung, and Blood Institute) as a division of the National Institutes of Health. The act also created the National Advisory Heart Council, whose mission was to review academic medical centers' grant requests for research projects and training programs. Braunwald observed, "It was no coincidence that the golden age of cardiology began soon after the National Heart Institute…was established in 1948. The federal commitment to biomedical research grew progressively, especially at the beginning of this period, and the Institute's budget rose from $16 million in 1950 to $1 billion in 1990." At the same time, the National Heart Act charged the NHI with providing grants to train clinical cardiologists in matters of diagnosis, prevention, and treatment of heart

Walter S. Priest, MD
ACC President, 1955 – 1956

Groedel and Reichert: Reflections on the Early Days

Franz Groedel was the driving force behind the founding of the American College of Cardiology but after his untimely death, co-founder Philip Reichert played an immensely important role in the development of the ACC because he helped lead the organization through its formative years and was still serving as executive director at the time William Nelligan stepped into that role in 1965.

Reichert's widow, Faith, still lives in the apartment at 480 Park Avenue where so much history was made and recalls with remarkable clarity many of the events of 50 years ago when the ACC was founded.

How did Groedel and Reichert meet? There are two first-hand accounts, and they are not mutually exclusive. In his memoir written on the occasion of the College's 30th anniversary, Reichert recalled that he and Groedel became friends after Reichert built a device for Groedel that provided "new information about the innervation of the heart muscle and the progression within the heart muscle of the stimulation in its course." Mrs. Reichert's recollection is that her husband had received an appointment as chief of cardi-

ology at Beth David Hospital in New York. She continues, "After about four months, the president of the hospital called him in and said, 'I have a very difficult question to put to you. Under what conditions would you give up your position to someone else? We love you, you're fine, we're not discharging you, but what if there was someone, a very famous doctor, who was of such importance that he would help the hospital and he will only accept a position as chief cardiologist?' Philip said, 'Groedel is the one man I would give up this job for.'"

Mrs. Reichert, who had her own career teaching history of costume design disease. As W. Bruce Fye notes in his book, *American Cardiology: The History of a Specialty and Its College*, "The creation of the NHI (and the funds it disbursed) had an immediate impact: the number of cardiology training programs and fellowship positions quadrupled in just five years."

Despite the changing – and highly favorable – dynamics of the era, the young ACC would survive only with hard work. Groedel was so dedicated to the new organization that he gave up his practice and devoted his office staff to the task of building membership. Those welcomed to membership became "Fellows" and were allowed to use "F.A.C.C." after their names. Soon, the ACC's leaders were spending their evenings sorting through hundreds of applications, a clear confirmation of the need for a practitioners' organization. Plans were put in place for a first meeting of the membership, and October 1951 was targeted as the date. Within weeks of the meeting, tragedy struck. Groedel fell, incurring a head injury that left him partially comatose and, within weeks, dead.

Simon Dack, MD
ACC President, 1956 – 1957

His passing was announced at the meeting by the man who would become his successor, Bruno Kisch, a strong leader who was well suited to take the reins. That first meeting attracted more than 275 physicians, and its program of scientific papers "covered the

at New York University, remembers returning from days at the university to meet her husband at Groedel's apartment. On several occasions she napped on Groedel's couch while Groedel, her husband, and others debated the need for a new society of cardiovascular specialists. She recalls, "The Americans in the group would say that the idea was silly because there was the American Heart Association, while Groedel would say, 'You Americans are ridiculous – we're not asking the public for money and we're not doing research. I want an educational institution.'"

Ultimately, the debate was resolved in favor of the forceful Groedel, and Mrs.

Reichert recalls doctors seated around her dining table deciding they needed $15 each to pay for incorporation. She continues, "Somebody had to take notes of what they were saying and the fact that each one was chipping in, so Philip said to me, 'You know how to type, come on and be the temporary secretary.' I made those notes, and I certainly didn't want to mix them up with our personal things, so I got a grocery box and put the papers in there. I kept it behind the draperies in the living room."

George R. Meneely, MD
ACC President, 1957 – 1958

medical and surgical management of heart failure, cardiac arrythmias, coronary insufficiency, myocardial infarction, arterial hypertension and rheumatic heart disease," according to Reichert. In planning the meeting, Kisch followed Groedel's precepts: that no lecture or demonstration be for the glorification of the speaker, that the material would be immediately useful to every physician in attendance, and that all should leave with knowledge that made attendance worthwhile. As Reichert said in an early history of the College, "If any single aspect of the program of the College ever stands out, that is it. The customers must get what they come for!"

As his term wound down, Kisch made another important contribution: expanding the leadership outside the New York area, which he did by turning over the presidency to Robert Glover, a Philadelphia surgeon. Glover's first priority was securing the financial position of the ACC. At his own expense, he hired auditors to set up a book-keeping system and decided a salaried office manager was needed. This goal was achieved in 1955, after Glover's term expired, when records were collected from Reichert's living room and Kisch's office in Brooklyn and consolidated at an office in the Empire State Building. Maude Crafts was hired to manage the

First awarded in 1961, the Groedel Medal
recipients to date include William B. Bean,
Sol Sherry, Eugene A. Stead, Jr., Leroy Hood.

office. Kisch's goal of a national organization was also enhanced by moving the ACC's meetings to locations such as Chicago, Kansas City, Los Angeles, and Washington, D.C.

In the meantime, the College made its entry into publishing. In 1951, the ACC initiated a monthly news bulletin that was distributed to all members, and it began semi-annual production of *Transactions of the American College of Cardiology*, which contained papers presented at the previous convention. With the rapidly expanding output of clinical and laboratory research reports that warranted distribution among the membership, *Transactions* underwent a major change within a few years. The College's Board of Trustees empowered Simon Dack (ACC president, 1956 – 57) to appoint a search committee to find an editor and publisher for a new, regularly issued periodical. The publication that emerged from this process was called *The American Journal of Cardiology* and was intended to be a teaching journal dedicated to practicing clinicians and cardiologists. Dack was named editor, and the first issue appeared in January 1958.

At the same time that the College's meetings were moving geographically to accommodate physicians from all parts of the

George W. Calver, MD
ACC President, 1958 – 1959

Philip F. Reichert in the ACC's offices in the Empire State Building, circa 1965.

country, format changes made them more useful for participants. One change was to hold two national scientific meetings – the annual meeting in the spring and what was termed an "interim" meeting in the fall. Both consisted of a single session; there would be no concurrent presentations until 1966. Scientific exhibits were introduced in 1953, commercial exhibits the following year. A novel idea, the "fireside chats" were introduced in 1955. As opposed to general session presentations, fireside chats brought small groups of doctors into contact with recognized leaders for learning on a more intimate scale. Ten or so physicians would sit at a table for exchange with a leading cardiologist. If the cardiologist's reputation was grand enough – the fireside chat could become "standing room only."

The idea of education for the practitioner took on another dimension as early as 1953, when one of the College's trustees suggested that something beyond large conventions was needed to promote involvement, exchange, and proximity. The answer was the "preceptor workshops," in which the ACC enlisted leading teachers to open their offices and laboratories to small groups of physicians for two- to three-day workshops. As Reichert noted in his 30th anniversary memoir, "The idea took hold at once. The best names in American medicine were swiftly enlisted. By 1955, we had a published list of 37; for 1956, there were 52; in 1957 more

Osler A. Abbott, MD
ACC President, 1959 – 1960

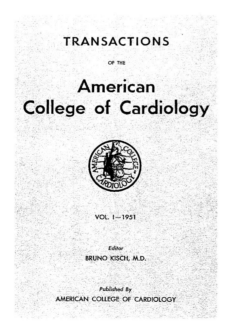

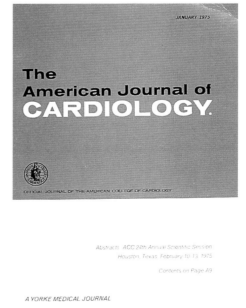

Transactions of the American College of Cardiology, containing papers presented at the previous national meeting, first appeared in 1951 with Bruno Kisch as editor.

The American Journal of Cardiology, a clinical research journal dedicated to practicing clinicians and cardiologists, was launched in 1958 with Simon Dack as editor. The issue pictured is from

1975. It was replaced as the College's official journal by the *Journal of the American College of Cardiology* in 1983.

than 70 were added. The concept was a coast to coast program scattered from January to December each year. One could choose one's subject, place and time. There was no fee for any of this. We were running a new kind of college course in postgraduate medical education – the first time anything like this had been offered…. The whole program was directly in line with the basic concept of the College."

Louis F. Bishop, Jr., MD
ACC President, 1960 – 1961

In 1961 William B. Bean was the first recipient of the Groedel Medal.

Paul Dudley White MD

USA 3

One of the pioneers of cardiovascular medicine, Paul Dudley White, was honored with a commemorative stamp by the U.S. Postal Service in 1986.

Vision to Reality

By the mid-1950s, the College as a national organization had embarked on the passage from vision to reality. Active recruiting, word of mouth, and geographic dispersion of meetings all were contributing factors. When the ACC leadership saw a hole, it acted to fill it. A case in point: The ACC's fifth president, Walter Priest, traveled to the West Coast in 1955 specifically to engage the cardiological community there. The strong response led to applications from leading West Coast cardiologists, such as Eliot Corday, Myron Prinzmetal, and George Griffith.

At the same time, there was a strong tailwind filling the new organization's sails and propelling it forward: a virtual explosion of knowledge and the awareness on the part of practicing cardiologists that they needed to stay current with new developments if they hoped to incorporate them in their practices. The founders had been almost prescient in their anticipation of this trend. From the beginning, Groedel had decreed that any ACC educational endeavor had to impart "a chunk of useful knowledge" to the practitioner cardiologist.

One of the early accomplishments of the College was not only to recruit members but to sell itself to those who were serious doubters. In an interview, Simon Dack recalled Louis Katz, a leading academic cardiologist who would become president of the AHA, challenging him over the need for another cardiological society. Paul Dudley White, perhaps the most widely recognized cardiologist of the era, steadfastly refused to join the ACC. Gradually, during the 1960s, the hostility waned and the legitimacy of the ACC prevailed. Ultimately, both Katz and White became honorary Fellows of the College.

As a new decade – the 1960s – opened, the reach of the ACC was about to expand significantly. Reichert wrote that the College was becoming recognized abroad "through the peregrinations of Fellows traveling to give lectures, talk about the rapid broadening of cardiologic knowledge here and the recognition of the 'F.A.C.C.' as a mark of distinction." A steady flow of applications for membership came into the United States from cardiologists in other parts of the world.

This worldwide growth begged the question, "What of continuing education for clinical cardiologists elsewhere in the world?" The answer came in the form of the International Circuit Courses. The concept was to have teams of cardiovascular physicians and surgeons travel to less developed countries to present advances in the practice of cardiology. The first International Circuit Course, funded by grants from the U.S. State Department and Eli Lilly pharmaceutical company, visited the Philippines and Taiwan in October 1961. It was led by Eliot Corday, E. Grey Dimond, C. Walton Lillehei, George Burch, and Simon Dack. "Eliot went to the State Department and sold them on the idea as a sort of

E. Grey Dimond, MD
ACC President, 1961 – 1962

Extending a hand to the world, the ACC initiated International Circuit Courses in 1961 with a mission to the Philippines and Taiwan led by E. Grey Dimond (far right). With him were Eliot Corday, George Burch (behind Dimond), Simon Dack, and C. Walton Lillehei.

Medical Peace Corps," Reichert recalled in his 1979 history. Some 2,500 physicians attended the sessions in Manila, and another 500 in Taipei, the second stop. The program traveled to 44 countries in its first five years, and won widespread praise.

An achievement of particular note occurred in 1973 when a team of eight doctors representing the ACC were invited to the People's Republic of China (PRC). The stage for this two-week international Circuit Course was set during meetings between U.S. Secretary of State Henry Kissinger and Premier Chou En-Lai of the PRC, both of whom made medicine and science priorities among the two countries' initial cultural exchanges.

John S. La Due, MD
ACC President, 1962 – 1963

An effort aimed at inspiring younger cardiologists was launched even before the ACC ventured offshore. In 1960, Dimond proposed a "Fellowship Award" – an idea that was quickly adopted as the "Young Investigators Award." He saw it as a way to encourage young heart specialists and to stimulate their interest in research through recognition. A $1,000 prize and a medal were offered, to which 26 researchers responded by submitting papers. Ten were

During the first International Circuit Course in 1961, Ferdinando Martires of the University of the East College of Medicine was presented with an ACC fellowship certificate by Ambassador John D. Hickerson. Those present for the ceremony in Manila, Philippines, includes Cultural Attache of the American Embassy George A. Rylance, Mrs. Martires, Ferdinando Martires, Ambassador Hickerson, Jose Cuyegkeng, Frederick Lim, and Cesar de Padua.

George C. Griffith, MD
ACC President, 1963 – 1964

Dwight E. Harken, MD
ACC President, 1964 – 1965

The International Circuit Course Program is introduced in Calcutta by C.L. Mukherjee, director of Health Services, Government of West Bengal, India. Members of the ACC team (from left) are George C. Morris, Jr., Charles A. Hufnagel, Forrest H. Adams, Albert Brest, and Harold T. Dodge.

selected to present their work at the first Young Investigators Award session at the 1961 meeting.

Eliot Corday, MD
ACC President, 1965 – 1966

An even larger educational breakthrough was in the offing. The constitution of the ACC had set forth the key objective of making available "free postgraduate training in cardiology and angiology." Based on the steady growth of its medical education programs, the College was doing a superb job of fulfilling this mission. The objective of "free" was becoming impractical, as Fye notes, "as the trustees sought to expand the number and scope of their continuing medical education offerings and attract academic cardiologists as speakers while keeping their dues in line with other professional organizations." Thus the College began to charge tuition fees in 1961, having already begun to reimburse speakers' travel expenses in 1959. Interest in continuing education gained momentum, with further impetus provided in 1965, when President Lyndon B. Johnson's Commission on Heart Disease, Cancer, and Stroke declared that "continuing education is a categorical imperative of contemporary medicine." At the same time, the possibilities for remote learning were enhanced considerably by the advent of slides and projectors and audiocassettes and recorders/players.

Around the World With the International Circuit Courses

It won't come as news to any member of the ACC who has served as faculty for the International Circuit Courses, but the world can be a dangerous place. To wit, the story of former ACC President Forrest H. Adams (1971 – 72).

He, his wife, and four other couples were on an International Circuit Course behind the Iron Curtain in Eastern Europe in 1965. (The other faculty members were George Morris, John Moyer, Henry Russek, and Albert Starr). They started in Yugoslavia, and after a few days they went to Budapest, Hungary, for a similar set of lectures.

The plan called for the group to then fly to Warsaw, Poland. Tensions between the United States and Poland had been running high, and when the group arrived at the Budapest airport they found their reservations had been "lost." Not to be put off, they left Budapest aboard the Orient Express and crossed into Czechoslovakia en route to Poland.

At the first stop, just inside the Czech border, guards boarded the train and told the doctors and their wives that they were being detained because they didn't have visas.

They were taken to a military outpost that mostly consisted of one large room. They weren't permitted to call the U.S. embassy, and it became apparent they were going to spend the night in jail. The doctors "bedded down" on the floor, their wives on wooden benches. Guards kept sentry all night.

The next morning, the doctors paid a small fine to gain their release and were taken back to the station to catch another train bound for Warsaw. Only with the help of another passenger did they figure out where to change trains and, after a full day's travel, they finally made Warsaw. The course turned out standing-room only crowds and was a huge success.

Dimond, who served as ACC president during 1961 – 62, combined these new media to meet the growing need for education in a novel way by initiating the American College of Cardiology Extended Study Services (ACCESS) in 1969. Dimond became ACCESS' first long-term editor. Directed specifically to the practicing cardiologist, ACCESS presented advances in diagnosis and treatment in the form of interviews and discussions led by the editorial board of ACCESS, excerpts from college-sponsored symposia, and summaries of published articles. Fye notes that "Introducing the first tape, an announcer told listeners that they should find the program useful whether they listened 'while relaxing at home, at the office, or perhaps use them to retrieve time otherwise lost riding in your car, or eating lunch.'"

C. Walton Lillehei, MD
ACC President, 1966 – 1967

Owing to the flexibility it offered doctors, the program was an immediate success. Within six months, there were 2,000 subscribers – only one-third of whom were ACC members. By 1974, that number had expanded to 4,600, and ACCESS had been renamed ACCEL™, for American College of Cardiology Extended Learning. The switch occurred in 1972, when it was learned that a corporation had copyright protection for the acronym ACCESS. Meanwhile, the program's first videotape made its debut in 1973. Today, ACCEL audiocassettes are distributed monthly to 8,000

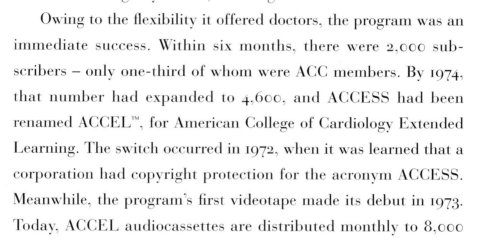

Vol. 5, No. 20   Internal Medicine News   11

To Lecture on Cardiology in Far East

These five physicians make up the faculty of the U.S. State Department-sponsored American College of Cardiology circuit course to be presented in Pakistan, Ceylon, Burma and Singapore Sept. 25 to Oct. 14. From left, the doctors are Samuel M. Fox III, professor of medicine, George Washington University School of Medicine and president of the college; Dean T. Mason, professor of medicine and physiology, and chief, cardiopulmonary section, University of California at Davis School of Medicine; W. Dudley Johnson, clinical associate professor of surgery, Medical College of Wisconsin, Milwaukee; H. J. C. Swan, professor of medicine, University of California Los Angeles School of Medicine, and director of cardiology, Cedars-Sinai Medical Center, Los Angeles; and Henry I. Russek, senior attending cardiologist, St. Barnabas Hospital, New York, and visiting professor in cardiovascular disease, Hahnemann Medical College and Hospital, Philadelphia.

subscribers who renew at an average rate of more than 90 percent. Moreover, ACCEL is but one dimension of today's broad-based extended learning program (discussed in more detail in subsequent chapters).

With its focus on meeting the needs of practicing cardiologists – and its considerable success at doing so – the ACC had moved to the center of the burgeoning field of cardiology. Yet, in the mid-1960s, there was some feeling of disquiet among the ACC leadership that, at least from a geographic perspective, the organization was more at the periphery. The locus was shifting to Washington, D.C. – the International Circuit Courses were arranged in cooperation with the State Department, discourse with NIH and other federal agencies was on the rise, and in 1965 Medicare and Medicaid were enacted into law. Was the organization's headquarters in New York City too far removed from medicine's new capital?

Increasingly, the answer was yes. Although the College had no governmental affairs arm at the time, its leadership believed it had a responsibility to inform members about pending legislation related to medicine and research. Members, in turn, were urged to communicate with their elected representatives. At the same time, any contemplated move had to take into account practical considerations. From the time the ACC was situated in the Empire State

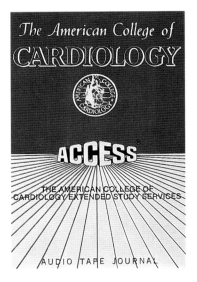

William Likoff, MD
ACC President, 1967 – 1968

The ACC explored new opportunities to fulfill its educational mission with the advent of audio-tapes and slides. American College of Cardiology Extended Study Services (ACCESS) first appeared in 1969. Within six months, there were 2,000 subscribers. In 1972, ACCESS was renamed ACCEL, for American College of Cardiology Extended Learning. A year later, the College's first video made its debut.

Building, Reichert had served as paid executive director and, for a number of reasons, he had no desire to relocate. In addition, there was a year's lease remaining on the office space. In addition to being centrally located, rents were less expensive in Washington, and the ACC would likely be able to acquire additional space.

As early as 1962 a committee had been formed to consider relocation. In 1963, a management consulting firm prepared a plan that identified a clear need for more precise planning and a revamped organization with expanded services. Thus, two issues coalesced: the desire to move to the nation's capital and the need for a full-time executive director to spearhead a broader agenda.

In his 30th anniversary memoir, Reichert recalls the moment: "For a College without walls, it was obvious that the central office had to be a symbol of continuity, as indeed it had for 15 years…. We had a smooth-running organization with a nice stack of money

George E. Burch, MD
ACC President, 1968 – 1969

The ACC Board of Trustees are shown as they assembled for a meeting prior to the opening of the ACC 19th Annual Scientific Session in 1970. Seated (left to right) Ray W. Gifford, Oscar Magidson, H.J.C. Swan as chairman of the Bethesda Conference, George E. Burch, B.I. Martz, William A. Sodeman, George C. Griffith, Alfred Soffer, and Forrest H. Adams. Standing (left to right) are Don W. Chapman, Harry F. Zinsser, Henry I. Russek, Louis F. Bishop, Archie A. Hoffman, Allan M. Goldman, Dwight Harken, Sylvan L. Weinberg, Warren J. Taylor, Robert W. Oblath, Ernest Craige, William D. Nelligan as executive director of the College, and Charles Fisch.

stashed away and little to worry about…[there was little need to] budge until the time was ripe. Then, suddenly, something happened that changed [this] attitude…and that something was Bill Nelligan."

William Nelligan, 39 years old, was executive director of postgraduate medical education at the Medical College of Georgia. His link to the ACC was E. Grey Dimond, who worked with Nelligan between 1955 and 1960 when Nelligan was in the University of Kansas Medical School's postgraduate medical education department. Dimond would like to have hired him three years earlier during his presidency of the ACC, but it was not until the strategic direction of the College was set in place that the opportunity presented itself. Nelligan came to the 1965 annual meeting in Boston, and he impressed the ACC's leadership. As if one more reason for

B.L. Martz, MD
ACC President, 1969 – 1970

William Nelligan, who served as the ACC's executive director for 27 years, was named a Fellow of the College upon his retirement in 1992. Here, he receives the Presidential Citation Award from the College in 1975.

moving to Washington were needed, Nelligan made it clear he preferred not to relocate his family to New York. With Nelligan's acceptance contingent on a Washington location, the ACC extended an offer. Nelligan accepted and an *ad hoc* relocation committee soon began scouting locations in the Washington, D.C., area.

William A. Sodeman, MD
ACC President, 1970 – 1971

President Richard M. Nixon received the ACC's Humanitarian Award in 1971 from ACC President William A. Sodeman. At left is J.C. Lungren, the president's personal physician.

In 1965, President Lyndon B. Johnson
changed the practice of medicine when
he signed into law PL 89-97 establishing
Medicare and Medicaid.

The Turning Point

Nineteen sixty-five would prove to be a pivotal year for the College, for cardiology, and, indeed, for all of medicine. Two defining events took place within a matter of weeks of each other: In June, the future role of the ACC was determined when the Board of Trustees voted to move from New York to Bethesda, Md.; in July, President Lyndon B. Johnson set the course for medicine when he signed Medicare and Medicaid into law.

Earlier in the year, Eliot Corday had created an *ad hoc* Office Relocation Committee and signaled ACC members that, along with education, closer relationships with the government and with federal agencies such as the NIH should be viewed as a central element in the society's mission. With Nelligan hired and the road to Washington cleared, the central question became precisely where in the national capital area to locate. While the issue of city versus suburb was debated at some length, Bethesda was eventually chosen for its proximity to the NIH complex and for the availability of campus-like settings affording a more academic environment than the hurly-burly of a central city.

The ACC set up headquarters in a stone mansion on the 11-acre campus of the Federation of American Societies for Experimental Biology (FASEB). The benefits of the move were confirmed for the ACC's leadership almost immediately. Fye points out in his book that former ACC President Samuel Fox observed that the new location "gave College leaders 'opportunities to engage in things with the federal government because we were right up the avenue, so to speak, from the headquarters of many of the relevant agencies.'"

Another debate was settled on July 30, 1965, when President Johnson signed PL 89-97 establishing Medicare and Medicaid. The idea of some form of national health insurance had been discussed since the late 1940s. Despite the opposition of many in the medical profession, with Democrats occupying the White House and firmly in control of Congress, it finally became reality.

The advent of Medicare, in particular, had a major effect on cardiology for two reasons: First, heart disease was especially common among the elderly, for whom the law was intended, and, second, cardiology was becoming more procedure and technology oriented. With years of research yielding new techniques, procedures, and equipment, the specialty of cardiovascular medicine was poised for explosive growth. How this growth was generated was not universally viewed as a development for the better. Bemoaning the effects of the procedure-oriented Medicare reimbursement schedule, former ACC President George Burch wrote in the *American Heart Journal* in 1977, "The cost of cardiac care needs careful scrutiny. The cost certainly can be reduced considerably, and primarily through better education of bedside cardiologists and physicians. Routine expensive 'tests' result in 'big money.'"

Forrest H. Adams, MD
ACC President, 1971 – 1972

The first Bethesda Conference, another major event of that seminal year of 1965, further cemented the new era of ACC – government cooperation. Congress was eager to see its considerable investment in medical research pay off in terms of application to practical needs. In light of the ACC's educational mission, Eliot Corday saw an opportunity for the College to help facilitate the flow of knowledge from laboratory to clinic. That was the concept behind the first Bethesda Conference, a two-day meeting of ACC members and officials of the Federal Aviation Agency, the Public Health Service, and United Airlines to examine pilots' physical fitness standards. A month later, in December, the second Bethesda Conference was convened with the objective of defining optimal training methods for saving lives in coronary care units. The first Bethesda Conferences won plaudits for the ACC on Capitol Hill and helped the College to realize that it had a legitimate role as a source of advice and counsel to the various agencies of the government. The Bethesda Conferences would prove to make lasting contributions to cardiovascular medicine. Through 1998, a total of 30 conferences had been held, producing reports on patient care, research, and training, as well as recommendations that would influence the future of cardiology. In particular, the conferences stimulated the development of standards and guidelines issued by the ACC as well as practice guidelines issued jointly by the ACC and the AHA.

Samuel M. Fox, III, MD
ACC President, 1972 – 1973

The success of both the move to Washington and the ACC's initial involvement with the government notwithstanding, the question now coming to the fore concerned the extent to which the College should be involved in governmental affairs. Only a few years earlier, the College's leaders had disavowed any such desire. An advocate of increasing dialogue with Washington, ACC President Eliot Corday established a legislative committee to confer with the government on matters relating to cardiology. Taking the opposite position, E. Grey Dimond felt that the AHA was the proper organization to maintain this relationship, in large part because it had performed in that role for more than a quarter century. Corday had the ACC's leadership on his side, however, and the committee went ahead. It was not a moment too soon, for Congress was about to embark on a period of legislative activism, enacting a number of new laws affecting cardiovascular specialists.

The ACC held its first scientific session in New York City in October 1951. Commercial exhibits were introduced in 1953. These pictures are from the Boston annual meeting in 1965. The ACC's Annual Scientific Session has become one of the world's premier international cardiovascular meetings.

H.J.C. Swan, MD, PhD
ACC President, 1973 – 1974

A plan takes shape. "A college without walls" found
a permanent home when ground was broken for
Heart House in 1975. Heart House was dedicated on
October 3, 1977.

Henry D. McIntosh, MD
ACC President, 1974 – 1975

Even today, the Learning Center (top) very much resembles this architect's rendering, created nearly 25 years ago.

This was a major concern for the College during this period for another reason – it heralded a change in the federal government's role, from funder of research to monitor of health care delivery. In the years after World War II, the powerful "heart lobby," led by Senator Lister Hill, Congressman John Fogarty, and business-woman Mary Lasker, served as a powerful advocate of increased government funding for research and the training of additional clinical cardiologists. Their involvement played a major role in the passage of the Heart Act. Another important voice during this period was that of Michael DeBakey, who, in 1966, would gain fame by implanting the first successful heart booster pump. DeBakey was a self-described "activist" in the heart lobby and a vocal advocate of academic research centers. By the mid-1960s, however, the government had become more attentive to health care delivery and the economics of medical practice. In 1964, DeBakey himself would chair a Presidential Commission on Heart Disease, Cancer, and Stroke, and, in an alliance with Hill, he helped secure passage of the Heart Disease, Cancer, and Stroke Amendment of 1965. Although the legislation had limited impact, it was indicative of increasing governmental involvement in medicine.

Charles Fisch, MD
ACC President, 1975 – 1977

In 1970, the ACC legislative committee's name was changed to the Committee on Governmental Relations, with Ohio cardiologist Sylvan Weinberg succeeding Corday as its chair. As the need to track, interpret, and respond to legislative developments became more important, the trustees hired Washington health care special-ist Ray Cotton, J.D., on a part-time basis to assist the committee. In 1981, the College established and staffed a full-time government relations department in order to have a resource dedicated to maintaining cardiology's interests in Washington.

As if the 1960s had not produced enough change for the ACC, one more landmark event was waiting in the wings: the purchase of land for what would become "Heart House." Nelligan had engi-neered a smooth relocation from New York to Bethesda and, from the start, events confirmed the wisdom of choosing the Washington area for the College's headquarters. But, just three years later, in 1968, the ACC was already outgrowing its offices. A burgeoning membership – soaring from 1,987 in 1960 to 4,305 by 1970 – required a steadily larger full-time staff. Moreover, the College's expanding role in governmental affairs, in addition to its primary educational mission, escalated the need for adequate facilities.

Office space for staff, while necessary, was not the primary stimulus that would ultimately transform a building into a magnet for cardiovascular specialists the world over. E. Grey Dimond conceived of a headquarters with a technologically advanced learning center that would go right to the heart of the ACC's mission and – as has been noted by many observers – change a "college without walls into one with walls." Dimond even had an idea for a name for the new facility: Heart House.

Dean T. Mason, MD
ACC President, 1977 – 1978

Participants in the second ACC Bethesda Conference on Coronary Care Units, held in December 1965, gathered for a photo on the steps of the College's first home in the National Capitol area, the Federation of American Societies for Experimental Biology (FASEB). The conference was led by Hughes W. Day (first row, far right), Eliot Corday (first row, far left), and Samuel M. Fox III (top row, fourth from right).

To become reality, inspiration still had to win out over practical matters – principally, of course, money. The first step was accomplished with comparative ease. In 1968, the trustees approved a resolution authorizing the purchase of a 9.8-acre site in Bethesda, near the NIH and the National Library of Medicine. The cost was $525,000, financed by a combination of funds in the treasury, an interest-free loan of $100,000, a $50,000 bequest, and a short-term bank loan. The second step – the building itself – proved to be more of a challenge.

In 1970, Dwight Harken was chosen to lead the fund-raising effort. The membership was divided over the merits of an ambitious ($5 million) building project. Some saw unnecessary financial risk. Others questioned how an East Coast location would benefit cardiovascular specialists in other parts of the country. Other objections ranged from desirability of several geographically dispersed learning centers to the reticence of physicians to rally behind fund-raising campaigns. Thus, it was not until 1975 – the

Leonard S. Dreifus, MD
ACC President, 1978 – 1979

This model of Heart House was created
by the architectural firm of Perkins & Will,
Washington, D.C.

ACC's 26th anniversary year – that ground was actually broken for Heart House. In the intervening years, the College mounted an energetic and far-reaching fund-raising campaign. Communications with members stressed the universal benefits of Heart House while countering arguments against it. The campaign reached out to foundations and industry as sources of financial support. In the midst of the effort, new teaching methods hinted at the promise offered by the Learning Center. For example, in 1973, the first ACCEL videotapes appeared, and the College sponsored a symposium on instructional technology. By 1976, Harken's campaign had reached the $4 million level, and Heart House was just a year from completion.

Borys Surawicz, MD
ACC President, 1979 – 1980

E. Grey Dimond and Dwight Harken try their
hand at turning a shovelfull of earth at
Heart House ground-breaking ceremonies in 1975.

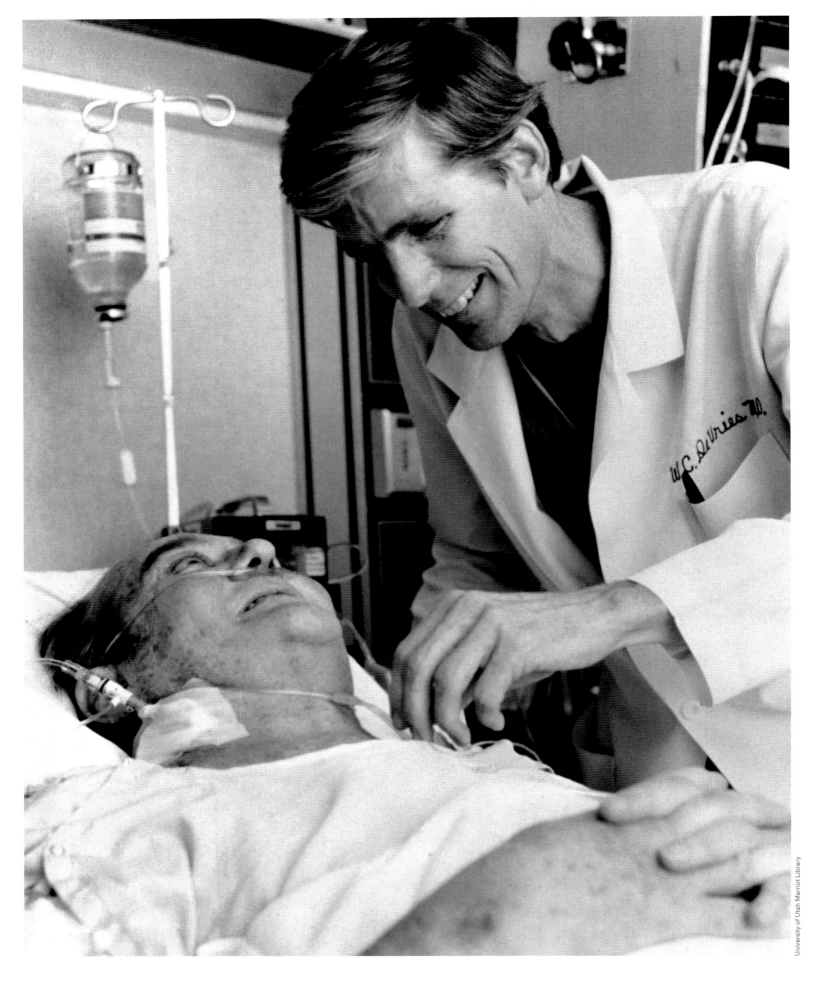

William DeVries monitors the progress of
Barney Clark, who, in 1982, became the
world's first recipient of an artificial heart.

Prosperity

Assessing the ACC's growth, Fye writes in *American Cardiology: The History of a Specialty and Its College*, "The rapid growth of the American College of Cardiology during the 1970s was a reflection of the vitality of the specialty it represented. Between 1965 (when the ACC moved to Bethesda) and 1979, College membership tripled, to 9,360, and the number of board certified cardiologists increased sixfold, to 5,228.... Many factors – social, political, economic, medical, scientific and technological – fueled the specialty."

Perhaps the crowning moment of the period came on October 3, 1977, when Heart House was officially dedicated in ceremonies presided over by ACC President Dean Mason and attended by some 900 members, friends, and supporters. The facility drew rave reviews. Reichert, in his 1979 memoir, recalled that "The greatest interest was shown in the wonderful space and equipment for teaching, learning and educational research. The big classroom had the latest in multimedia communications aids. The room had 67 learning stations, each with a chair with an armrest console, which had a five-channel TV monitor, multiple choice response system, a stethephone, palpator, call light and tape recorder jack. Each custom designed classroom chair had on its back a small brass plate with the name of the donor of the chair. A student will not just listen to a lecture; he will see close-up a chart or electrocardiogram, actually hear a heart beat and be able to feel a pulse. Continuing postgraduate education has here a model that we hope will shortly be copied everywhere."

In May, a few months before the dedication, Heart House had been occupied by the administrative staff, who found ample office space. Having a headquarters not only brought staff together under one roof, it also provided a controlled environment for higher quality teaching and learning as well as conference rooms for committee meetings and events such as the Bethesda Conferences. Moreover, Heart House provided a collegial atmosphere – from coffee breaks on the terrace to conversations around the fireplace in the winter. Showcase features of the new building included specialized spaces later named the Griffith Resource Library and the Dack Atrium, as well as a series of "named" conference rooms. Originally, Dimond had envisioned the inclusion of living accommodations, but that dimension of Heart House never came to pass, as the College elected to house Learning Center students in nearby hotels.

Two weeks after the dedication, Heart House hosted its first course in the Learning Center. Devoted to the subject of auscultation, the course was entitled "The Bedside Art and Science of Cardiac Diagnosis" and was led by former AHA President W. Proctor Harvey and Antonio de Leon, Jr., both of Georgetown

Robert O. Brandenburg, MD
ACC President, 1980 – 1981

Heart House Television was the power behind the scenes in the early days of the Learning Center. Beginning in the mid-1980s, Heart House Television came into its own when it produced its first broadcasts and teleconferences. It became a stand-alone operation in 1992.

University Medical School. Once the Learning Center was in use, it more than lived up to expectations. While the advanced technology grabbed most of the attention, the smaller size of the Learning Center compared with large medical school or convention center lecture halls created a more intimate environment for learning. Nearby break-out rooms permitted personal interaction in a small group setting. For the faculty, the Learning Center was a teacher's dream. In addition, scholars were able to use individual rooms in the Griffith Resource Library for private study. Today, the library's staff performs more than 800 literature searches annually.

Dan G. McNamara, MD
ACC President, 1981 – 1982

ACC/AHA practice guidelines, familiar to all ACC members today, first appeared in 1980, springing from an idea generated a few years earlier by former President Charles Fisch. They were then and are now published in the *Journal of the American College of Cardiology* and the AHA's *Circulation*, and both organizations equally share representation and costs. At the time, there was a growing sense among the leaders of the ACC that the federal government and third-party payers wanted some form of practice

In the Learning Center, instructional media is not only educational. It can be fun as well.

Suzanne B. Knoebel, MD
ACC President, 1982 – 1983

Paul A. Ebert, MD
ACC President, 1983 – 1984

The Learning Center: the heart of Heart House. A breakthrough facility, the Learning Center was a forerunner in multimedia communications aids. Today, each chair is a "mini-learning center" housing a TV monitor, multiple-choice response system, a stethophone, palpator, call light, and tape recorder jack.

guidelines; and if the College didn't undertake to write them, someone else would. The College approached the AHA with the idea that the guidelines should be developed and published jointly, as they would then carry the weight of two preeminent cardiologic organizations.

John F. Williams, Jr., MD
ACC President, 1984 – 1985

In 1982, the Board of Trustees of the College made the decision to sever ties with the publisher of its then-official periodical, *The American Journal of Cardiology*, and created a new official journal owned by the ACC. That decision led to the debut of *Journal of the American College of Cardiology (JACC)* published by Elsevier Science Publishing Co. With the new journal, the College's long-time editor in chief, Simon Dack, planned to step aside but with considerable urging agreed to stay on. A few years after *JACC* made its appearance, a survey of members found it was rated the primary benefit of ACC membership.

Journal of the
American College
of
Cardiology

Elsevier Biomedical

In 1983, the College introduced a journal
that it owned, *Journal of the American College of
Cardiology (JACC)*.

Two vastly different events marked 1985. Sadly, the last direct tie to the ACC's founding circle was lost when Philip Reichert died. Some years earlier, in 1966, he had been chosen to receive the College's first "Distinguished Fellow" award. Of him, Louis F. Bishop, Jr., wrote, "It was Phil Reichert's dedication, administrative skills and enthusiasm which led the College in its early years on the path of education of the academic and clinical cardiologist." The second event reflected the College's ongoing growth. A 29,000-square-foot addition to Heart House was completed and dedicated. The new wing provided additional office space and a dining facility for use during Learning Center programs.

William W. Parmley, MD
ACC President, 1985 – 1986

Throughout this period, the federal government was increasingly making its presence felt on the legislative and regulatory front. The ACC, which had mobilized in the area of government relations in the early 1970s, became increasingly active itself, seeking to ensure that its voice was heard in the corridors of power. With the turn of the decade, the government became even more aggressive on issues of cost, access, and quality. ACC President Suzanne Knoebel (1982 – 83) spent many hours testifying on Capitol Hill and urged the College to develop "consensus statements" on cardiovascular

Philip Reichert received the College's first "Distinguished Fellow" award in 1966. The last direct tie to the ACC's founding circle was lost when he passed away in 1985.

practices and procedures, lest they be dictated by others. During the mid-1980s, the ACC urged members to pay more attention to the socioeconomic aspects of cardiology practice.

Today's chapter structure can be traced to this period and to concerns over government regulation of cardiovascular medicine. The first state chapters had been established in the years following the College's founding in 1949. However, ACC President Ashton Graybiel did away with them in 1954. He believed that at that early stage in its development, the ACC would be better served if it consisted of a single national organization unencumbered by the more localized needs of state chapters.

By the mid-1980s, state laws were beginning to have a major impact on health care. The ACC had a health policy team at the federal level but no way to track legislation and regulation at the state level. In 1986, a group of Florida heart specialists moved to form a state-level association in order to be represented in the Florida Medical Association. For the leadership of the ACC, the implications of such an action were clear: the possibility of independent organizations throughout the country and a setback for the College as the central organization representing cardiovascular

John Ross, Jr., MD
ACC President, 1986 – 1987

ACC President Suzanne B. Knoebel (1982 – 83) frequently testified on Capitol Hill during a period when the government expanded its role in medicine. Here she is testifying with Edwin P. Maynard of the American College of Physicians and Roy Schwarz of the American Medical Association.

specialists. ACC President William Parmley and ACC Executive Vice President William Nelligan convinced the Florida doctors that the better choice was for the ACC to form a state chapter with which they could affiliate. Thus, the ACC's chapter structure was reborn, with Florida and Arizona becoming the first two. With the advent of chapters, the focus of the Board of Governors broadened from membership and credentialing issues to include state regulations and socioeconomic issues. The number of chapters expanded rapidly through the 1980s. Today, there are 37 chapters representing 41 states.

Francis J. Klocke, MD
ACC President, 1987 – 1988

Yet another major step in government relations occurred in 1986 when the ACC developed a "key contact" program to familiarize College members with federal policies on subjects such as NIH funding, health care delivery, and physician reimbursement and to give physicians a stronger voice on Capitol Hill. The ACC's government relations department organized meetings between College representatives and key members of Congress in order to present the ACC perspective on matters related to cardiovascular

Chapter Relations Committee members and staff meet at ACC '90 in New Orleans. Left to right: Mary Beth Gilovitch, Lita Watson, Adolph M. Hutter, Jr., Nora F. Goldschlager, Michael A. Nocero, Jr., Harold Smulyan, William D. Nelligan, William W. Parmley, William H. Frishman, Donald J. Jablonski, Bertram Pitt, Richard P. Lewis, Rebecca Trachtman, Edward D. Frolich, Charlene May, Cary Kuhlman, William L. Winters Jr.

research and practice. In the early 1990s, the key contact program mobilized to express concerns about the new electrocardiogram reimbursement policy and was instrumental in its repeal. The key contact program continues today at the federal level, and some chapters are organizing efforts at the state level as well.

Other initiatives included the annual Legislative Conference, first held in 1989 in Washington, D.C. The conferences provided the opportunity for College members to meet in person with representatives of government and the private sector. Today, the Legislative Conference emphasizes a two-way exchange of views on a broad range of health care topics. In 1990, the College launched an initiative to communicate regularly with members about government relations activities through a monthly newsletter, *Washington Update*. Today, a weekly summary of events is posted on the ACC's Web site. Underscoring the importance of

Anthony N. DeMaria, MD
ACC President, 1988 – 1989

The ACC's William Nelligan and Robert Levy, director of the National Heart, Lung, and Blood Institute (NHLBI) in 1975. In the late 1970s, the ACC and the NHLBI were drawn into the debate over the effects of the Carter administration's commitment to "cost containment and quality assurance."

government policy decisions, the ACC's Annual Scientific Session includes a Health Policy Symposium.

American College of Cardiology

Washington Update

Where to turn for legislative and regulatory news

Volume 4, Number 6   June 1998

Poll Finds Americans Want Congress to Protect Their Health Care Rights

Americans expect quality from their health care plans, and they are willing to pay a reasonable amount more to ensure access to the specialists, treatments, and information they need to make sound judgments about their own health. Furthermore, Americans believe that because managed care plans are not providing these protections, it is time for Congress to step in and protect patients' rights.

Those are among the key findings of a poll recently released by the Patient Access to Specialty Care

Coalition (PASCC), of which the American College of Cardiology (ACC) is a member. The poll tested the six principles that comprise the Patient Choice and Access to Quality Health Care Act of 1998 (H.R. 3547), a bill introduced by Reps. Dave Weldon, R-Fla., and Sherrod Brown, D-Ohio.

The nationwide poll of more than 1,000 Americans showed that the principles in H.R. 3547 are overwhelmingly popular with the American people. Frank Luntz, of Luntz Research Companies, who

conducted the poll, said at a May 14, 1998, press conference that in all of his years of polling he had not seen an issue with such universal numbers that cut across party, age, and income lines.

The poll found that nearly 97 percent of Americans would support legislation that requires health care providers to give their patients full information about their conditions and treatment options. Access to in-network specialists and the right to a speedy appeal when a plan denies

Continued on page 2

ACC President Sends Urgent Message on Tobacco

American College of Cardiology (ACC) President Spencer B. King, III, MD, has issued a call to action to all members of the ACC in response to the Senate's failure to pass a comprehensive tobacco control bill before the Memorial Day recess. This effort is an attempt to counter a well-funded tobacco industry initiative that has resulted

in thousands of calls to Capitol Hill opposing the tobacco bill.

In his May 26, 1998, letter, Dr. King told his colleagues that cardiovascular specialists "must demand that the Senate continue consideration of tobacco control legislation first thing upon return on June 1." On May 18, the Senate began

Continued on page 3

INSIDE
College Supports McCollum Bill 3
Patient Confidentiality Issues 5
ACC Addressing Medico-Legal Issues 5
In Brief 6
State Affairs 7
Physician Data Collection Moves Forward 8
Legislative Tracking 14
State Tracking 18

printed on recycled paper

C. Richard Conti, MD
ACC President, 1989 – 1990

In 1990, the College launched *Washington Update* to communicate regularly with members about government relations activities. A weekly version is now available on the College's Web site.

Gene chips, such as this one photo-
graphed at the Genetics Institute,
may open a wholly new way to diagnose
and treat cardiovascular disease.

New Issues, New Ways

As the 19th century turned into the 20th and cardiology began to assume a distinct and recognizable form, a whole new vocabulary emerged: the electrocardiograph, the sphygmomanometer, X-rays, the Nauheim bath, the cardiac clinic, and a host of new laboratory techniques.

Over the course of the century, cardiovascular medicine would see cardiac catheterization, open heart surgery, pacemakers, coronary angiography, the coronary care unit, coronary artery bypass graft surgery, echocardiography, percutaneous transluminal coronary angioplasty (PTCA), heart transplants, artificial hearts, and much, much more. Now, on the edge of the 21st century, there are equally new fields that are once again transforming cardiovascular science. Molecular biology and genetic engineering are the most promising and far reaching. But there are ongoing advances across a broad front, from new techniques in echocardiography to development of new antithrombolytic agents.

Throughout this period of constant, accelerating change, the ACC remained focused on high-quality continuing medical education to keep the cardiovascular specialist current and to help raise standards of practice around the world. Just as the vocabulary of cardiology has changed, so has the lexicon of education, as video, CD-ROM, and the Internet affect the way subjects are taught and information is communicated.

Worldwide, the most visible single element in the College's multidimensional educational program is the Annual Scientific Session. Today, it is the world's premier international cardiological meeting, drawing more than 30,000 registrants from nearly 100 countries. Independent surveys have found that for nearly 60 percent of registrants, the Annual Scientific Session is the only cardiological exposition they attend. (Refer to the sidebar on page 72 for a profile of a recent Annual Scientific Session.) A comprehensive educational program covers every key area of cardiovascular medicine, including basic research, prevention, clinical decision making, and the latest treatments. Meeting highlights include presentation of about 2,300 abstracts, a complement of symposia and other sessions permitting in-depth learning in a small group environment, international symposia on global cardiovascular issues, and sessions that present real-world clinical practice issues through patient case studies.

William L. Winters, Jr., MD
ACC President, 1990 – 1991

In 1996, 30 years after the ACC first offered simultaneous scientific sessions, the College's site on the World Wide Web made its debut. Education via the Internet is still in its formative stage, but the opportunities are limitless, especially the Internet's potential for addressing physicians' top problem with continuing education – time pressures. Already, ACC/AHA practice guidelines are posted on the World Wide Web, as are highlights from the Annual Scientific Session.

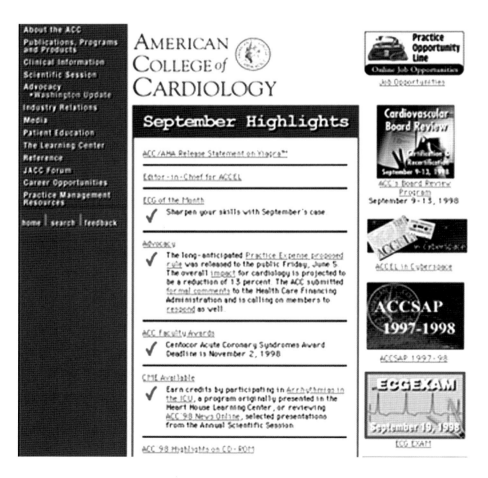

The ACC has had a site on the World Wide Web since 1996. Internet-related opportunities going forward are limitless. Already, ACC/AHA practice guidelines are posted on the site.

While traditional print publishing has been the backbone of the College's communications efforts, the Internet and CD-ROM technology have opened up new channels of communication, most notably for the *Journal of the American College of Cardiology*, which is continually rated as the best-read journal among cardiologists. *JACC* is available online as well as on CD-ROM.

Reflective of the greater emphasis on time, speed, and convenience, the ACC/AHA practice guidelines have undergone significant changes as well. Originally, the process of issuing a practice guideline required two years or more. That process has been reduced to 12–18 months, in spite of the fact that the ACC and the AHA have reached out to other organizations for participation. The guidelines have also been broadened to include cardiovascular conditions, not just procedures.

Robert L. Frye, MD
ACC President, 1991 – 1992

Beginning with the release of the practice guideline on acute myocardial infarction in November 1996 (and again with the congestive heart failure guideline), a teleconference was held to disseminate information. The goal was to make it as easy as possible for a 100-page document to become useful in day-to-day practice. A pocket version of a practice guideline first appeared in November 1997.

Throughout this period, another communications medium – Heart House Television – served as an invaluable resource. Heart House Television grew up supporting the Learning Center, but it came of age in 1986 when it produced its first external event by transmitting procedures being performed live at Georgetown University Hospital back to the Learning Center. In 1991, Heart House Television produced its first nationwide video satellite teleconference. Originating in San Diego and at the Learning Center with segments from four other locations, the four-and-one-half-hour teleconference, entitled "Echo in the Nineties," was sent to four sites, where more than 1,000 physicians had gathered. Concurrently, Heart House Television began producing the popular "Learning Center Video Highlights" videotapes and the "Learning Center Video Seminar Series." Over the years, Heart

House Television has produced more than 70 titles and distributed more than 100,000 tapes.

Although still primarily devoted to supporting the Learning Center, Heart House Television became a stand-alone operation in 1992. Through the balance of the decade, it moved into CD-ROMs, developed extensive medical graphics capabilities, and produced educational content for the ACC's Web site. In 1998, Heart House Television initiated a new "Learning Center Video Roundtable," a panel discussion format series of videos in which the participants discuss timely subjects related to cardiovascular medicine. Now, it is experimenting with digital video discs (DVDs), which offer expanded programming flexibility and storage capacity. Longer term, it is exploring the potential of three-dimensional virtual reality media.

Adolph M. Hutter, Jr., MD
ACC President, 1992 – 1993

While new media are making their impact, a traditional form of learning – the extramural program – continues with the Annual Scientific Session and seminars at Heart House to form the foundation of the College's educational program. The roots of this program can be traced back to 1955, when the ACC sponsored a hugely successful one-day symposium in New York on the subject of acute myocardial infarction. During the same era, College-sponsored events included visits to cardiac clinics and catheterization laboratories, as well as other small group sessions. Gradually, extramural programs emerged and took on the size and shape of today's program. Currently, more than 30 programs are held annually, with total attendance in the range of 7,000. Two have been held for more than 30 years: The oldest and largest, the New York Cardiovascular Symposium, attracts more than 1,000 physicians. In early 1999, the Cardiovascular Conference at Snowmass (Colorado) marked its 30th anniversary. Extramural programs are instrumental in preparing physicians for numerous cardiovascular board exams, including the Adult Cardiology Board Review, the Electrophysiology Board Review, and, as of 1999 the Interventional Cardiology Board Review. The ongoing success of the extramural program is attributed to expert faculty, state-of-the-art topics, a focus on clinically relevant material, excellent interaction with faculty and peers, and attractive city and resort locations.

—•—

Education has always meant information, but today's information technologies are reshaping the concept of education and broadening its definition. Recognizing that information access is to the future what education was to the ACC's founding, the College has developed – as a new line of business – a system for collecting and distributing data useful to hospitals and physicians. After several years of development and refinement, the College set up the American College of Cardiology National Cardiovascular Data Registry™ (ACC-NCDR™) in 1997. The initial ACC-NCDR effort is focused on catheterization laboratories and collecting case-specific data on PTCAs and catheterization. The ACC-NCDR's hospital participants collect the data, aggregate it, and send it to the College, which analyzes it and issues a report addressing 141 different elements. Reports focus on cath lab practices and outcomes, including complication rates, lesion data, patient demographics, and trending.

Sylvan L. Weinberg, MD
ACC President, 1993 – 1994

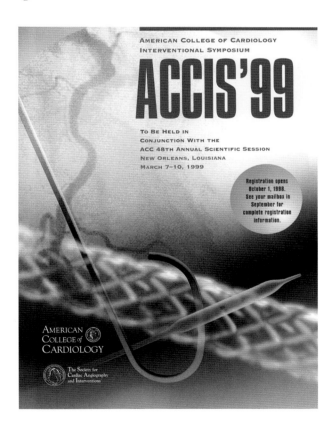

Today, the Annual Scientific Session offers a wide range of focused learning opportunities. An example is ACCIS '99 – the ACC Interventional Symposium at the 1999 meeting in New Orleans.

While the ultimate direction of this venture has yet to be determined, it is clear that information is driving the future of health care, and the ACC should be involved. The initial effort is hospital oriented, but it could easily move into the physician's office in the future. Likewise, the ACC-NCDR's work thus far is focused on selected procedures, but it could readily be expanded to offer data on additional procedures as well as major conditions, such as congestive heart failure or myocardial infarction.

Daniel J. Ullyot, MD
ACC President, 1994 – 1995

During the 1990s, the health care cost/quality debate continued unabated. Although their medical and scientific achievements were spectacular, cardiovascular specialists were easily singled out owing to their orientation to procedures and reimbursement under a traditional fee-for-service system. The ACC gradually learned that the critical, life-saving nature of its members' work was not enough to ensure it a voice in the national health policy debate. As the 1990s unfolded, the ACC assumed a more active advocacy role on behalf of heart specialists as well as their patients. The ACC started out with a small, outsourced government relations function. Today's efforts, by comparison, are strategic in nature and led by three committees and several task forces supported by an experienced government relations staff. Two newer committees that are augmenting the work of the Government Relations Committee are the Private Sector Relations Committee and the Economics of Health Care Delivery Committee. The former addresses issues related to employers and the private sector insurers, while the latter has played a critical role by providing information leading to the development of the resource-based relative value scale used by both the public and the private sector. Beginning in 1995, task forces were formed to address new issues as they arose.

As the century entered its final few years, the greatest health care policy issue for the ACC was the redistribution of resources from specialists to primary care physicians. The ACC takes the position that quality care is not being served by drastically cutting such essential services and is actively communicating its perspective to those formulating or influencing policy at all levels of government.

In 1996, the ACC began to review its relationships with industry. There were two outcomes – the simultaneous establishment of a Corporate Liaison Board and a Development Committee. The Corporate Liaison Board consists of 12 representatives from pharmaceutical companies and medical device manufacturers, who serve on a rotating basis. This board is the formal mechanism for communications between the College and industry, and it seeks feedback on ACC programs, gathers and shares information on industry trends, and brainstorms new initiatives aimed at improving patient care. The Development Committee is responsible for corporate- and member-giving programs, corporate relations, endowment programs, and other special revenue-producing activities. The Development Committee spearheaded the effort to secure financial support for the ACC's multifaceted commemoration of its 50th anniversary – the College's first fund-raising effort since Heart House was built.

J. Ward Kennedy, MD
ACC President, 1995 – 1996

In 1997, the Board of Trustees approved a comprehensive, new strategic plan. This action reaffirmed a commitment to effective planning that began in the late 1970s, when the College developed its first set of goals and objectives under the leadership of Charles Fisch. The College's first strategic plan was developed by a committee chaired by Robert Frye and was approved by the Board of Trustees in 1987. It set forth a number of goals that helped guide the College through the late 1980s and early 1990s. The 1997 strategic plan, developed under the leadership of George Beller, reflected the enormous changes that had occurred in governmental policies as well as the growth of international cardiology. Evolutionary rather than revolutionary in nature, it affirmed the existing mission statement, stressed the need to measure progress against objectives, and set the tone for the direction of the College as it moved toward the 21st century.

———◆———

While external relationships with constituencies central to cardiovascular medicine's future were of high priority for the College, evolving membership considerations occupied internal discussions during the 1990s. One of the ACC's chief concerns was meeting the needs of women practicing cardiovascular medicine. One issue was the number of women in the specialty; in 1990, only 5 percent of the nation's cardiovascular specialists were women.

The ACC's strategic plan supports "the principle of diversity in its committees and leadership roles. This includes encouragement of participation of qualified women and minorities in the College." An Ad Hoc Task Force of Women in Cardiology was created, and it took on two tasks. The first was the development of an ACC expert consensus document on Radiation Safety in the Practice of Cardiology (published in March 1998 in *JACC*). The second was the development and compilation of a survey of women and a representative sample of men in the ACC to identify the areas of professional and personal life that were of concern to women and men. The "ACC Professional Life Survey" manuscript was published in *JACC* in September 1998. In March 1998, the task force was elevated to full committee status, renamed the Women in

Richard P. Lewis, MD
ACC President, 1996 – 1997

In recent years, some 400 companies have exhibited at the Annual Scientific Session.

Cardiology Committee and chaired by Marian Limacher. Among the committee's activities, it is planning a leadership/professional development workshop at Heart House.

International membership also grew as an area of attention for the College. International members of the ACC have remained relatively constant at around 10 percent. However, about 40 percent of the attendance at the Annual Scientific Session today is from the international community and an even higher percentage of articles submitted to *JACC* comes from international scientists and cardiovascular specialists. The Credentials Committee has been working to revise membership guidelines to recognize individual academic cardiologists who are leaders in their respective countries and who possess the American equivalent of board certification.

Richard L. Popp, MD
ACC President, 1997 – 1998

In 1998, the Credentials Committee created a new class of ACC member – "Master of the American College of Cardiology" – created to recognize those individuals who, over a period of at least 15 years, made extraordinary contributions to the College. In addition to other individuals selected for this honor by the Board of Trustees, the designation was extended to all former presidents (and to outgoing presidents in the future). The other classes of membership remain Affiliate-in-Training, Affiliate (Temporary), Member, Associate Fellow, Fellow, Fellow Emeritus, Distinguished Fellow, and Honorary Fellow.

———— ◆ ————

Today, the ACC is a large and complex organization. It is governed by a Board of Trustees composed of 31 ACC Fellows and Masters elected by the membership and an eight-member Executive Committee. The board is responsible for ACC policy development, administration, and general management of the organization. The president of the ACC, elected for a one-year term, chairs the Executive Committee and the Board of Trustees. The Board of Governors consists of 67 representatives, including all 50 states, Puerto Rico, Canada, Mexico, and the uniformed services. Some 80 percent of ACC members are also affiliated with chapters. Around the world, there are ACC members in some 90 countries.

The real work of the ACC is performed in its committee structure, which today actively engages more than 500 volunteer physicians serving on 60 committees and on numerous task forces.

There are about 160 staff members organized under an executive vice president, who reports to the Board of Trustees. In 1998, the Board of Trustees selected a new executive vice president, Christine W. McEntee, under whose leadership the ACC has expanded to include six staff divisions. They are Education; Strategy, Finance and Operations; Clinical Practice and Scientific Services; Advocacy; Information and Online Services; and Human Resources and Organizational Development.

Spencer B. King III, MD
ACC President, 1998 – 1999

As Bruce Fye observed in his history of the College, "During its first century, cardiology emerged as one of American medicine's most significant specialties. Cardiology's growth was fueled by the prevalence of cardiovascular disease, the federal government's desire to blunt the societal and economic impact of these disorders, an impressive series of procedural and technological innovations, its image as a dynamic and exciting field, and favorable reimbursement policies. Despite dramatic changes occurring in the structure and financing of medical practice in the United States, cardiolo-

The Annual Scientific Session:
A Snapshot

The 47th Annual Scientific Session was held in March 1998 in Atlanta. A profile of participation shows the degree to which this event has become a magnet for health care professionals and cardiovascular specialists the world over, as well as exhibitors and representatives of industry and the media.

- Total attendance – 30,264
- Professional attendance – 17,049
- Number of exhibiting
  companies – 400
- Media representatives – 325

- Abstracts received – 5,969;
  abstracts accepted – 2,280
- International professional attendance – 6,710
- Countries represented (outside
  United States) – 94
Greatest professional attendance
by countries other than the United
States:
- Canada – 775
- France – 627
- Germany – 427
- United Kingdom – 418
- Brazil – 414
- 51 countries were represented by no
  fewer than 15 registrants

Leading categories of professional
attendance were:
- Physician/scientist (MD/PhD) – 13,101
- Nonmedical – 1,496
- Nurse/nurse practitioner – 1,284
- Paramedical – 829
- Trainee/resident – 773

gists will likely retain their key role in the care of people with serious and symptomatic heart disease."

The College itself is equally sanguine about the future. Its 1997 strategic plan declares, "By almost every measure, the American College of Cardiology is and has been a healthy and productive organization…. The College is as strong and vibrant now as it has ever been and remains an essential voice for the cardiovascular specialty."

Continuing to look ahead, the College remains committed to its members, their patients, and society. In its strategic plan, the College's first goal is set forth in these words: "Remain the primary professional association for all cardiovascular specialists in the United States." In identifying professionalism as a core value, the strategic plan asserts unequivocally, "The interests of the patients are primary."

Arthur Garson, MD
ACC President, 1999 – 2000

Half a century after the College was founded, virtually everything had changed, yet nothing had changed. Addressing his colleagues in 1949, Franz Groedel commended them for choosing "to meet the future not merely by dreams, but by concerted action… and inextinguishable enthusiasm." Today, his praise would be equally well placed.

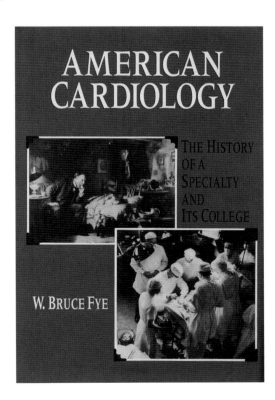

W. Bruce Fye, a Wisconsin cardiologist, teacher, and College trustee and historian, researched and wrote *American Cardiology: The History of a Specialty and Its College*, an in-depth book on the growth and development of American cardiology and the ACC. It was published in 1996.

Teaching

Professor Emeritus W. Proctor Harvey, MD

ACC: A Portrait

In any view of history, the story of the American College of Cardiology – indeed, of cardiology itself – is but a fleeting moment in time. Yet, in less than a century, cardiovascular medicine has emerged, grown, and flourished the world over. Matured it has not. Moreover, if its brief history is any portent of the future, it never will. If anything, the pace of change is accelerating as medical science transforms the diseases and disorders of the past into tomorrow's triumphant headlines. The people drawn to the challenges of this discipline understand that change is a powerful force leading to growth, innovation, and continuous renewal. Indeed, the ability to change is often the factor that distinguishes successful organizations from those that lose their relevance. The mandates of change keep the ACC focused on the future. While addressing a broad range of regulatory and economic issues, the College remains dedicated above all to the continuing education of the cardiovascular specialist – a mission that becomes only more relevant and more critical with each medical advance. Today's ACC is 24,000 strong, making it one of medicine's largest professional societies. The ACC's members include adult cardiologists, cardiovascular surgeons, pediatric cardiologists, teachers, and researchers. They are found throughout the United States and North America and in 96 different countries. Once a specialty unto itself, cardiology today embraces a growing range of subspecialties, and the ACC is responding with an ever-broader educational agenda. On the pages that follow, a series of photographs captures some of the diversity in cardiovascular medicine as it is practiced on the edge of the next millennium. Fifty years hence, when the College celebrates its centennial, will these scenes seem as quaint and curious as a patient in a Nauheim bath at the turn of the century? We leave that for the next generation to decide. For now, we celebrate a most remarkable 50 years.

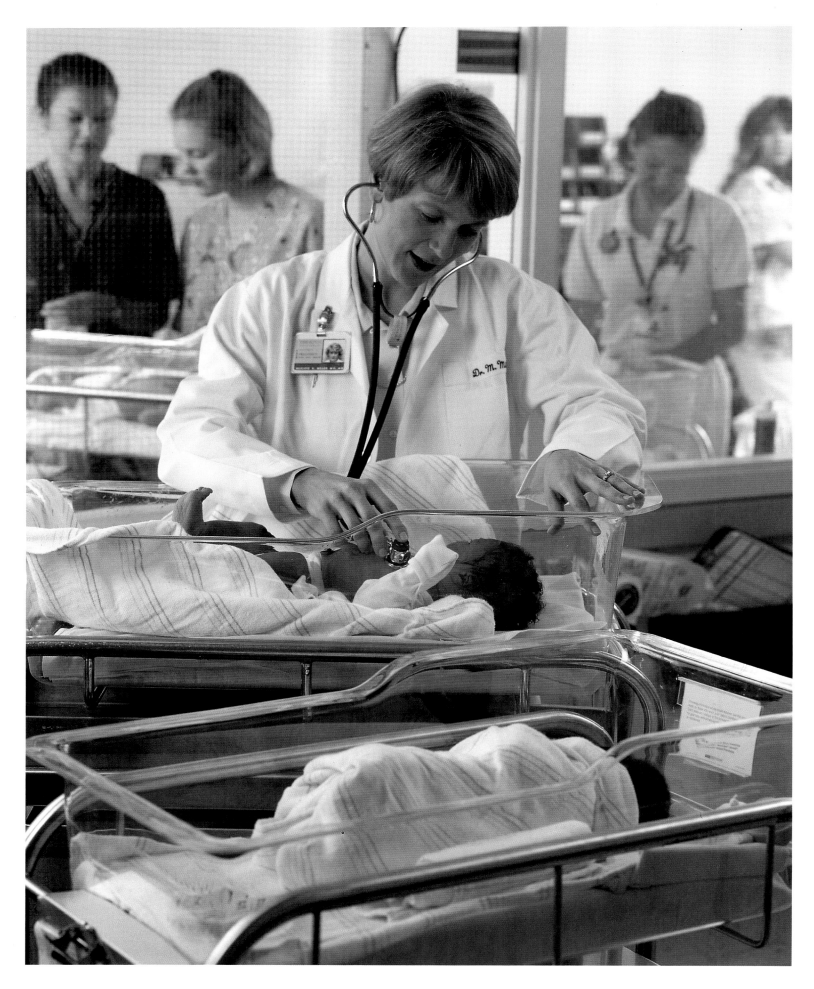

Pediatric cardiology
Marlene Miller, MD, PhD candidate,
fourth-year fellow

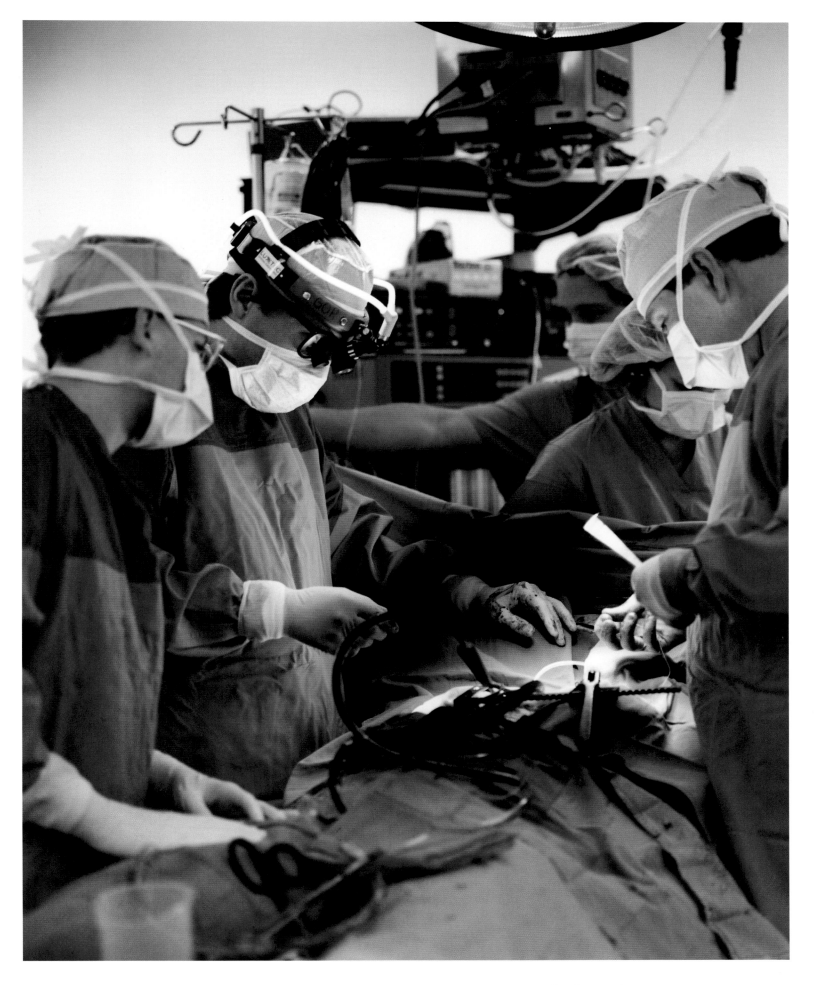

Cardiovascular surgery
Peter J. Gruber, MD, PhD, first-year fellow
J. Mark Redmond, MD, attending surgeon
John Liddicoat, MD, third-year fellow

University research
J. Michael Mangrum, MD, third-year
fellow, electrophysiology

Preventive cardiology
Susan J. Zieman, MD, second-year fellow

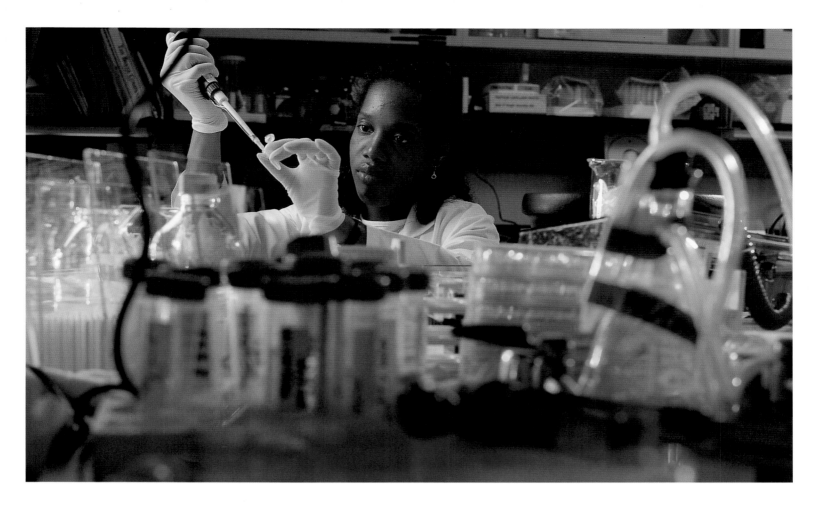

Basic research
Ramona Gelzer-Bell, MD,
second-year cardiology fellow

Nuclear cardiology
Tina M. Sias, MD, fourth-year fellow
Jeffrey Graham, technologist

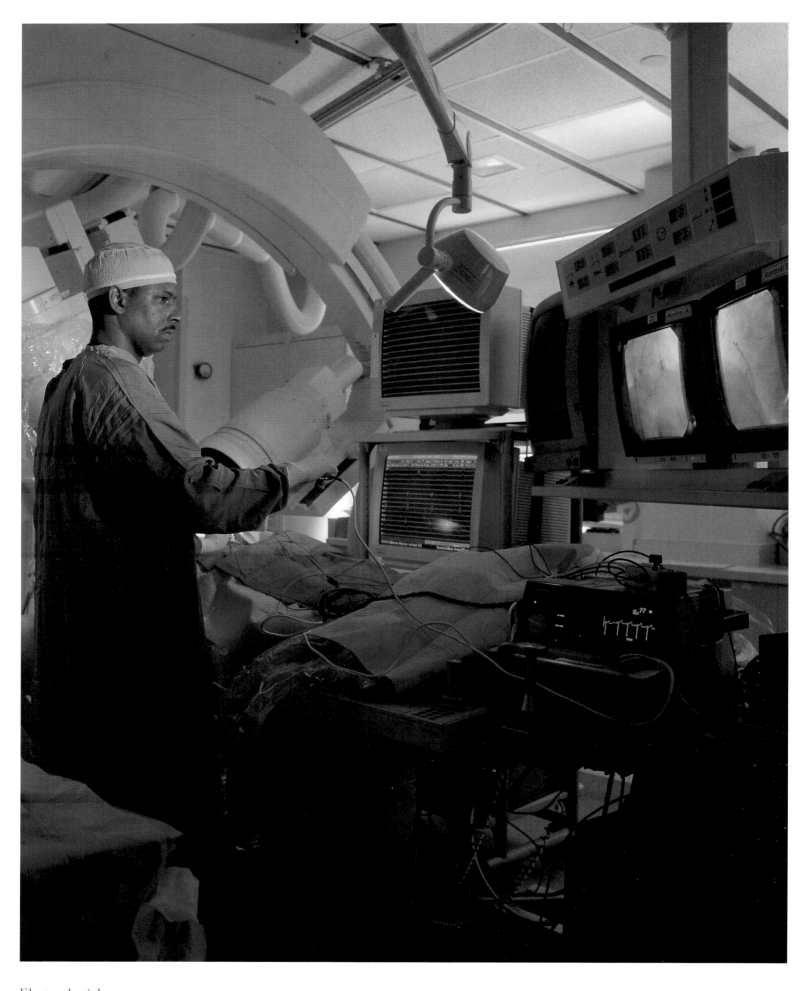

Electrophysiology
Eric Taylor, MD, fifth-year fellow

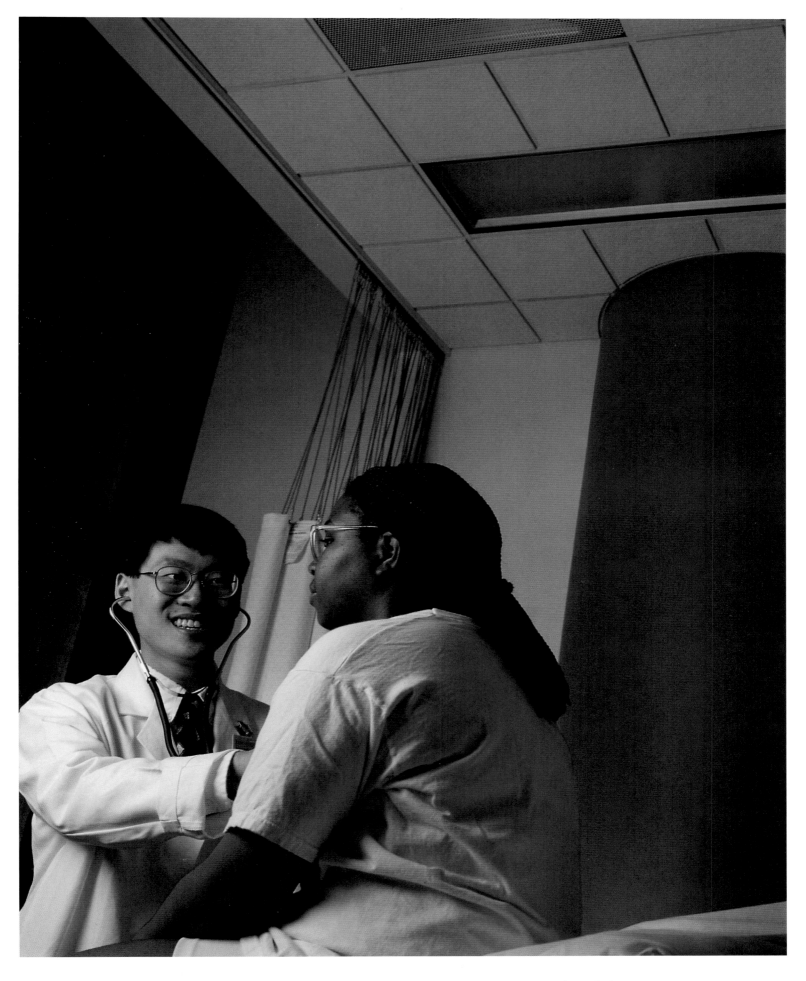

Adult cardiology
George Juang, MD, second-year fellow

Federally funded research
Daniel L. Dries, MD, MPH,
NHLBI fellow, advanced heart failure
and cardiac transplantation

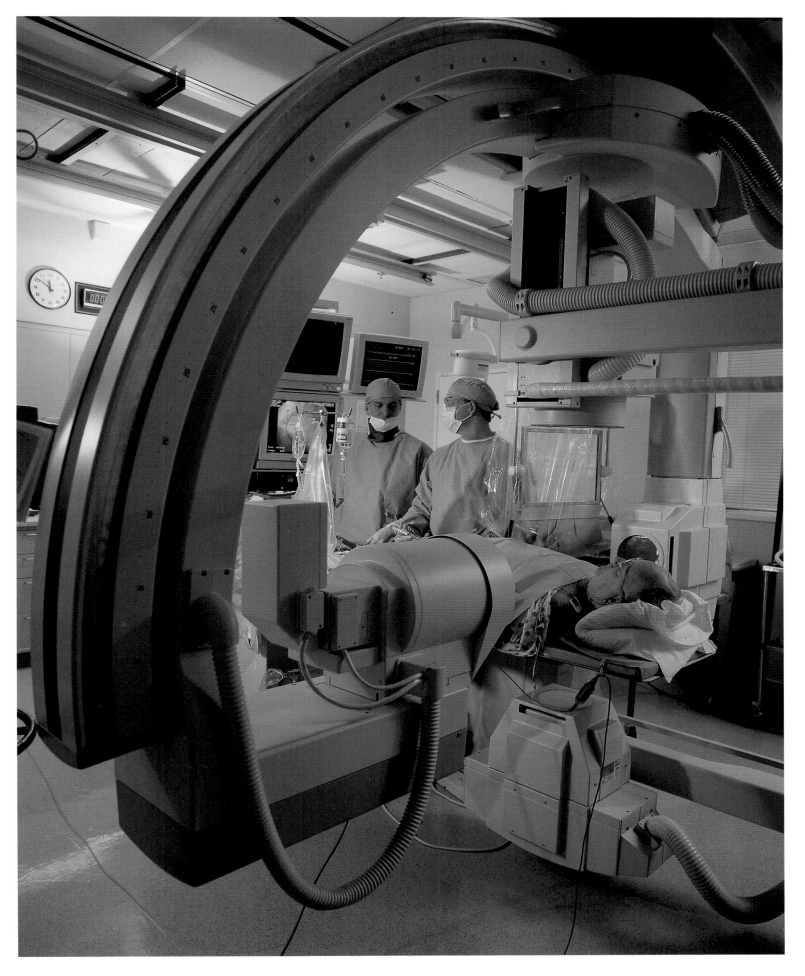

Interventional cardiology
John A. McPherson, MD, third-year
fellow, Michael Ragosta, MD, attending
cardiologist

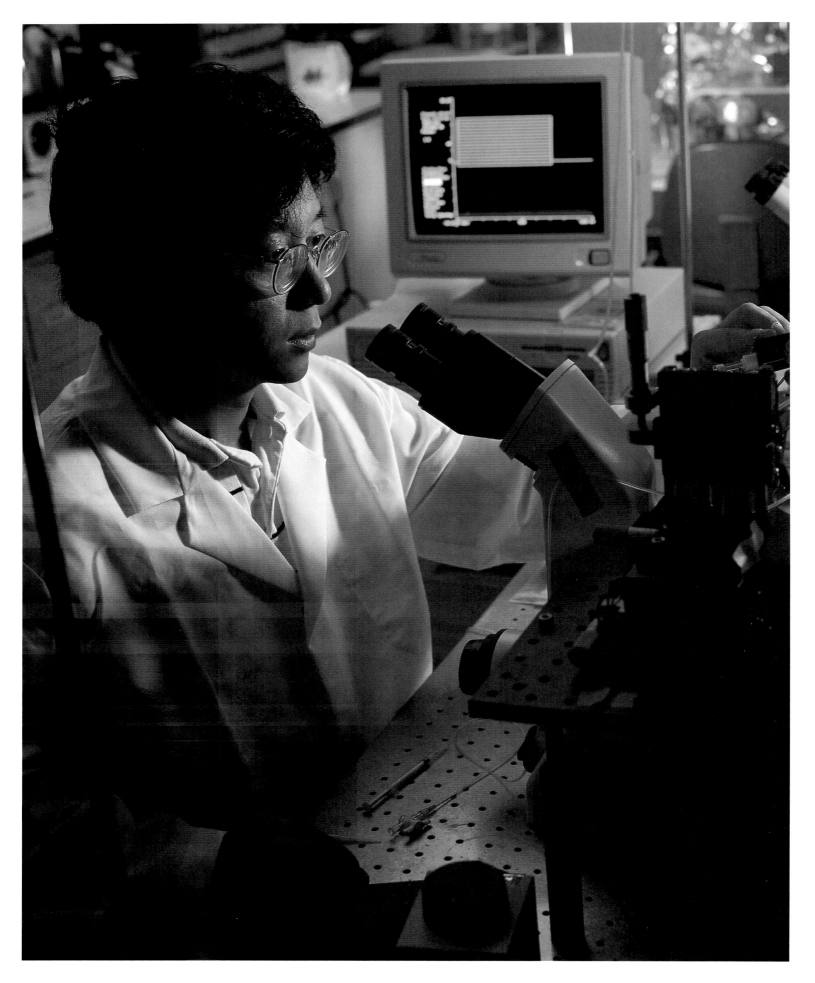

Industry research
Scientists from the private sector
collaborate with cardiovascular specialists.
continuing to make progress in the
diagnosis and treatment of heart patients.

ACC and Industry: A Shared Vision for Better Patient Care

Fifty years ago, the founders of the American College of Cardiology had a vision for an educational organization that would become a pillar for cardiovascular care. Through the efforts of those who carried on this vision and those who have supported it, the College has been and will continue to be the leader in cardiovascular care and education into the next millennium.

It is in the spirit of a shared vision for better patient care that the ACC gratefully acknowledges a select group of its industry partners and business suppliers for their generous support of the College's ongoing educational activities and its 50th Anniversary Commemorative Program.

In appreciation for their support and for their contributions to the advancement of cardiovascular medicine, the College recognizes its 50th anniversary sponsors:

Visionaries

 ASTRA Astra Pharmaceuticals

 Hoechst Marion Roussel

 NOVARTIS

 Bristol-Myers Squibb Company

 Roche Hoffmann-La Roche

 Pfizer U.S. Pharmaceuticals

 DUPONT

 Medtronic

 Procter&Gamble PHARMACEUTICALS

Genentech, Inc.

 MERCK

 RHÔNE-POULENC

 GUIDANT

SEARLE

Innovators

Centocor Inc.

Explorers

Cordis, a Johnson & Johnson company

Mallinckrodt, Inc. • Nycomed Amersham

SmithKline Beecham Pharmaceuticals • Wyeth-Ayerst Laboratories

Leaders

ATL Ultrasound, Inc. • Elsevier Science Inc.

Fujisawa Healthcare, Inc. • Marquette Medical Systems

Ground Breakers

CLB Printing Company • CPU, Inc. • DCP Graphics Corporation

Decatur Press, Inc. • Hyatt Regency Bethesda

MJH Associates • Pharmaceutical Media Inc. • Smith Litho

Afterword

"Although predicting is perilous, not predicting is even more perilous. It leaves us unprepared to the changes going on right under our noses, confronts us with recurrent surprises and makes us reactors instead of agents of change."

– Jerome Kassirer

Predicting the next hundred years is relatively simple; predicting the next 10 is very difficult. In 1980, I was asked to predict the next ten years of our field and then was held accountable in 1990 when I was asked to give a talk (called "Back to the Future: Part II") summarizing the success of my predictions. My range finding was off: Two of the predictions have just begun to occur 18 years later. Undaunted as to prediction, I do believe there will be changes in three important areas in the next millennium: in our practice, in our physicians, and in our health care.

Our practice will become more focused on prevention. The prevention of coronary artery disease and stroke by manipulation of molecular and mechanical factors is likely to precede the prevention of cardiomyopathies, heart failure, and congenital heart disease. Molecular diagnosis will precede molecular treatment; nonetheless, conventional treatments will be more productive with earlier warning provided by molecular diagnosis.

Long before these more global advances, incremental advances will move toward noninvasive assessment of the coronary circulation, minimally invasive approaches to coronary artery diseases, and application of molecular techniques to enable focused regeneration of myocardium and specialized conducting tissue.

Transplantation immunology and ethics will need to advance significantly to address issues of animal organs or growth of human tissue *in vitro*. Just as restenosis has spawned new research into Iatrogenic disease, so will every new treatment require investigation and treatment of its unintended consequences.

Our physicians will return to more cognitive pursuits as preventive strategies increase. In the short-to-medium term, however, there will be a need for the clinical molecular biologist (perhaps *cum* interventionalist) who will translate the new knowledge and apply it more rapidly than ever before. Our physicians will return to their traditional role as patient advocate; the preoccupation with cost will diminish. Cost will be only one parameter: Only those diagnostic and therapeutic regimens that significantly improve patient care at a reasonable cost will survive.

Our health care system will change. The Baby Boom generation is rapidly approaching the time when illness will visit them. This influx of an aging population will increase the overall cost of health care. Also, perhaps less obviously, the need for performance improvement and improved quality will lead to an increase in the cost of care. Americans, when presented with quality data that they understand, will choose the best health care available. This need for quality will cause a return to a more appropriate balance of specialty care than has been espoused in the past few years. The development of new technology, including molecular diagnostics and therapeutics, while improving the quality of life, will be expensive in both their development and their practice: They will prolong life but will still require some degree of health care services. This increase in cost will not be borne easily by the current private payers for health care, likely resulting in less coverage and more disenfranchisement of greater segments of the population. Traditionally, the United States has provided health care coverage for those least able to pay, beginning with the elderly and the disabled and extending to the poor. In the future, it will be the middle class who will be disenfranchised. The ultimate solution will require health care coverage for all Americans.

One future prediction is certain: The American College of Cardiology will continue to be the most relevant provider of medical education, performance improvement, and advocacy for those concerned with cardiovascular disease. If even a few of the changes I have outlined come to fruition, the knowledge deficit and the role for the cardiovascular specialist in helping to shape the health care system will become even more acute; the American College of Cardiology will be the agent for the practitioner in these areas. The College, building on its current and future membership, will be even stronger after its second 50 years than it is even after its amazing first 50 years.

Arthur Garson, Jr., MD, MPH, FACC
President-Elect, American College of Cardiology

Acknowledgments

The American College of Cardiology would like to acknowledge the many groups and individuals who made this book possible:

ACC Fellows Thank you to all of the ACC members who were available to help with the writing of this book, especially the Commemorative Book Working Group of the Subcommittee for the Commemoration of the ACC 50th Anniversary: W. Bruce Fye, chair; H.J.C. Swan; John F. Williams, Jr.; and William L. Winters, Jr. Also, Forrest H. Adams, Kenneth L. Baughman, William A. Baumgartner, George Beller, David J. Feild, Arthur Garson, Jr., Bernard J. Gersh, W. Proctor Harvey, Timothy D. Henry, Sharon Ann Hunt, Spencer B. King, III, and Sylvan L. Weinberg.

ACC Staff Thank you to all of the ACC staff who helped bring this project to fruition, especially Macon Ayers, Kathy Boyd, Melanie Caudron, Karen Collishaw, Jane Cosper, Karen Durland, Helene Goldstein, Marcia Jackson, Barbara Kendrick, Christine McEntee, Marie Michnich, Penny Mills, Gwen Pigman, May Roustom, Betty Sanger, Carolyn Thompson, Rebecca Trachtman, Elizabeth Wilson, and everyone on the ACC Support Services staff.

Friends Thank you to all of the ACC's friends who provided facts and images, especially Faith Reichert, Elaine Russek, Genentech, Inc., and Hoffmann-LaRoche, Inc.

Photography For the photography in the stakeholders section, thanks go to Robert Reichert and his team and to all who made the photography possible: Daniel L. Dries and Georgetown University Hospital; Marlene Miller, Peter J. Gruber, J. Mark Redmond, John Liddicoat, Susan Zieman, Eric Taylor, Ramona Gelzer-Bell, George Juang, and The Johns Hopkins Medical Institutions; John A. McPherson, Michael Ragosta, J. Michael Mangrum, Tina M. Sias, and the University of Virginia Health Sciences Center.

The Creative Team Many thanks to the design team at CONTEXT: Edvin Yegir, Peter Johnson, Kathleen Land, Tom Morin, Jeanine Caruso, Esmee Snyder, and writer Charlie Rhudy for their skill, creativity, and hard work.

A very special thank you A very special thanks to William D. Nelligan, whose amazing institutional memory was indispensable to the completion of this book.

The ACC also acknowledges Douglas P. Zipes and Richard P. Lewis, chairs of the Development Committee and its Subcommittee for the Commemoration of the ACC 50th Anniversary, respectively, from whose members the idea for this book originated.